The Complete Guide to Miniature Pinschers

Megan Grandinetti

Publication Data

Miniature Pinschers

The Complete Guide to Miniature Pinschers – First edition.

Summary: "Successfully raising a Miniature Pinscher Dog from puppy to old age" – Provided by publisher.

ISBN: 978-1-952069-98-7

[1. Miniature Pinschers – Non-Fiction] I. Title.

This book has been written with the published intent to provide accurate and author-itative information in regard to the subject matter included. While every reasonable precaution has been taken in preparation of this book the author and publisher expressly disclaim responsibility for any errors, omissions, or adverse effects arising from the use or application of the information contained inside. The techniques and suggestions are to be used at the reader's discretion and are not to be considered a substitute for professional veterinary care. If you suspect a medical problem with your dog, consult your veterinarian.

Design by Sorin Rădulescu

First paperback edition, 2020

TABLE OF CONTENTS

CHAPTER 12

INTRODUCTION

I am not a veterinarian, a professional breeder, or a dog trainer. I am just someone who spent five and a half years loving and caring for a very special Miniature Pinscher. His name was Brady.

Brady

At the time when I adopted Brady, I was living a solitary, unhappy life in a career that I absolutely hated. I had an idea that I'd adopt a medium-sized dog that could go running with me in Central Park. Then I met Brady, the overweight, senior Min Pin that changed my life.

At seven years old, Brady was in bad shape. He was not the svelte running buddy I imagined. But the minute I met him, I knew he was my dog.

Brady inspired a lot of change in my life. I started setting boundaries at work and coming home at a more reasonable hour because he needed me to look after him. I left my electronic devices at home and took him on endless walks and hikes. I started to see that work wasn't everything, despite what my bosses and clients wanted me to believe. I ended up leaving my career in Manhattan and found us a more spacious, better lifestyle in my hometown in Pennsylvania.

Brady stayed with me through all of it. Anywhere I went, he went with me. And if I left him to travel, he always jumped right into my arms the minute he saw me. That bond—between dog and dog owner—happens once in a lifetime, if we're lucky.

I never saw myself as a "small dog" kind of woman. But Min Pins are not small dogs. They have the biggest, brightest personalities of any dogs I have ever met. Brady was loved by everyone in my life. He was incredibly smart. He was loyal and loving. He was a jokester and a clown, and he made me laugh every single day.

Spending five and a half years as Brady's dog mom was not only one of the best privileges of my life, but it also gave me real insights into ownership of a Miniature Pinscher.

CHAPTER 1
About the Miniature Pinscher (a.k.a. the Min Pin)

What Is a Miniature Pinscher?

The Miniature Pinscher, also known by its German name as the *Zwergpinscher*, is a small, smooth-coated dog considered to be a toy breed. Miniature Pinschers, or Min Pins, are known as the "King of the Toys," and for good reason. These compact dogs are as regal as their nickname and elegant appearance implies. Although Min Pins are usually no taller than 12 inches and usually no heavier than 8-10 pounds, they are sturdy, dynamic dogs that are full of "big dog" personality.

Photo Courtesy of Anca Iusan

*Photo Courtesy
of Jacqueline Siotto-Zwirn*

History of the Min Pin

The Miniature Pinscher is a small breed of dog of the Pinscher type, with its origins in Germany. The Min Pin's ancestors may have included the German Pinscher, mixed with Italian greyhounds and dachshunds. Although it is often assumed that Min Pins are related to the Doberman Pinscher, based both on appearance and on name, this is a common misconception: the two breeds are completely unrelated.

The Min Pin was originally bred in Germany as a ratter, a dog for hunting vermin (primarily rats) in homes, barns, and stables. Because of their small size, they could get into holes and other small spaces that bigger dogs couldn't while chasing rats.

Experts think that the Min Pin breed could be several hundred years old, but there is no clear answer as to its exact age. In the United States, the American Kennel Club first introduced the Min Pin in 1929.

Photo Courtesy
of Marina Ivanova

Physical Characteristics

Miniature Pinschers are compact, sturdy dogs, most no taller than 12 inches and no heavier than 8-10 pounds. There are also Teacup Miniature Pinschers, which are about half the size of normal Min Pins.

Min Pins are athletic in build and are known for their high-stepping, or "hackney" (horse-like) gait.

A Min Pin's coat is short, smooth, and shiny, with no undercoat. The American Kennel Club (AKC) breed standard for colors is (1) solid clear red, stag red (with intermingling of black hairs); (2) black with sharply defined rust-red markings (on cheeks, lips, lower jaw, throat, twin spots above the eyes, and chest, lower half of front legs, inside of back legs, lower portion of hocks and feet, and black pencil stripes on toes); or (3) chocolate with rust-red markings (same as specified for black Min Pins, except a brown pencil stripe on toes). In both the solid red and stag red Min Pins, a rich, vibrant medium to dark shade is preferred.

My Min Pin, Brady, was black with rust markings. When we met, he was so overweight that friends joked that it looked like someone stuffed a sausage inside the body of a Min Pin. Or that he looked like a football with tiny legs and a face. On his first vet visit, he weighed more than 18 pounds! However, with the proper diet and a lot of exercise, he eventually grew into the trim, athletic, happy Min Pin he was always meant to be.

Behavioral Characteristics

"Min Pins are smart, curious, loving and are notorious escape artists. They need an owner who understands that they are not a lazy purse dog. They love to snuggle and cuddle but if given the chance they will run. A Min Pin is a perpetual toddler: inquisitive, smart, and they love human interaction."

JACQUELINE SIOTTO-ZWIRN
Sidels Miniature Pinschers

Miniature Pinschers are loyal, fun-loving, and playful. They are fearless, vigorous, and always alert, probably a leftover trait from their early days when they were bred for hunting. Min Pins are generally wary of strangers, bark at new people and noises, and make excellent guard dogs.

Because they have so much energy, Min Pins need a lot of exercise and attention before they're able to truly relax. In addition to being energetic, Min Pins are very smart, focused, curious, and strong-willed. Beware: due to their high intelligence, they are capable of dubious tricks you'd never imagine based on their size.

Take Brady and the curious mystery of the three-foot-tall step-lid stainless steel trash can. On more than one occasion, I'd come home to a toppled

Photo Courtesy
of Erin Wolfe

over trash can, with the contents strewn about the kitchen and picked over, as if Brady had hosted a garbage picnic while I was gone. But how on earth could that little man (who wasn't even as tall as my knee), knock over a round trash can that was three feet tall and needed someone to step on it to open it? His teeth marks gave a clue. Brady was smart and creative enough to step on the pedal to open the lid, sink his teeth into the trash bag, pull with all his little, tiny might until the entire can fell over,

FUN FACT

The Miniature Pinscher Club of America, Inc. (MPCA)

The MPCA has been an AKC Member Club since 1930. Among the club's objectives are encouraging responsible breeding and protecting the interests of the breed by encouraging sportsmanship at competitions. The MPCA has a quarterly publication, Pinscher Patter, available free for members and for a price for nonmembers. More information can be found at www.minpin.org.

and then rush out of the way so he didn't get crushed by the weight of it. Timber! And then he'd have a trash picnic. That's how clever Min Pins can be.

Min Pins also may be prone to separation anxiety. When I first adopted Brady, I worked long hours and had to leave him at doggy day care a few days a week. Every day, when I dropped him at the door, he would howl and cry like I was leaving him forever. Eventually, he would settle in for the day and enjoy himself with the other dogs and daycare staff. And every night, when I picked him up, he spun in circles and jumped with such excitement that I could barely get his harness around him. The separation anxiety was tough to adjust to at first, but it just endeared him to me more.

Because Min Pins tend to be both fearless and prone to anxiety, they are not always the best match for young children, who can be unpredictable and full of loud noises. And because of their small size, Min Pins are not well-suited to living with toddlers or kids who are rough with dogs, since they're more likely to get hurt (or fight back and hurt a child). For this reason, families with children should consider getting a Min Pin as a puppy so that they can raise and socialize the young dog from the beginning. Min Pins generally do well with older children and teenagers, as well as adults.

Depending on the level of socialization they are exposed to as puppies, Min Pins may or may not get along well with other dogs, due to their alpha personality. Socializing early helps to ensure good behavior. Because of their breeding, most Min Pins will go after small animals, such as mice, rats, and hamsters. Cats may or may not be an issue.

Is a Miniature Pinscher the Right Dog for You?

How do you know whether a Miniature Pinscher is the right dog for you? Are you looking for a dog that will:

- *Want to go wherever you go?* Min Pins are prone to separation anxiety, so they are happy to go wherever their owners are and should not be left constantly alone.

- *Make you laugh each day?* Min Pins can be fun-loving, playful, and fierce little jokesters.

Photo Courtesy of Barbara Farrell

Photo Courtesy
of Nicole Gray

- *Be completely portable?* Because of their small size, Min Pins are completely portable. You can even carry them in bags on public transportation, if you so choose.
- *Be 100% protective of you and your family members?* Min Pins make great guard dogs, and they are willing to protect their owners at any cost.
- *Enjoy walks, hikes, adventures, and games?* Min Pins have a lot of energy, so they are game for all types of exercise.

And likewise, are you the type of owner that will:
- *Be a strong and kind pack leader?* Min Pins are "alpha" dogs, so they need an owner that will take charge and show them who's boss.
- *Give your dog enough exercise and attention?* Min Pins have a lot of energy, so they tend to need a couple of good walks per day, plus some games to keep their natural curiosity at bay.

If the answer to these questions is "yes," you're ready to be an owner of a Miniature Pinscher. Congratulations!!

If you answered "no" to any of these questions, particularly about giving your dog enough exercise, attention, and leadership, perhaps you should explore a more laid back and less energetic breed.

CHAPTER 2
Choosing a Miniature Pinscher

"Miniature Pinschers are well suited to most any home. They are a high energy breed so they need plenty of exercise, either daily walks or a fenced in yard to run in. They also do very well with children, as long as they are raised with children in the home."

KAREN MERICA
Lilbears Kennels

Photo Courtesy
of Olesya Deryabina

Buying vs. Adopting

There are two main ways to find your ideal Min Pin: buying one from a reputable breeder, or adopting one from a rescue organization. A big benefit to adopting a Min Pin instead of buying one is that there is a dog out there that is waiting for a home, and you could save that Min Pin from euthanasia. You could also adopt a Min Pin that is older than a puppy, so you may miss out on the crazy puppy behavior. Your rescue Min Pin might already have a bit of basic training and could require less work (training, socialization, exercise, etc.) than a brand new puppy from a breeder.

CELEBRITY MIN PIN
Dollar Hilton ★★★★

American media personality Paris Hilton is the proud owner of a Min Pin named Dollar. Hilton adopted the puppy in June 2013. Shortly after adopting Dollar, Hilton posted an adorable close-up of the puppy on Instagram and encouraged her followers to adopt instead of shop with the hashtag #Adoptdontshop.

There are also some downsides to adoption that shouldn't be overlooked. A rescue Min Pin might have a lot of issues: health, behavior, or otherwise. Sometimes dogs end up in rescue organizations because they have health issues that their owners can't afford to deal with. Other dogs are put up for adoption because of behavioral problems—they might have bitten someone or didn't get along with a family member. And still, some other perfectly healthy, well-behaved dogs end up homeless because their owners pass away, move, or have a child and can't care for their dog.

All that said, there is something magical about a brand new, 8-week-old puppy from a reputable breeder. Not only will you be able to know, from the breeder, what kind of health your Min Pin is in, but you'll also have peace of mind that the puppy hasn't been through any underlying trauma that would create behavioral issues. Furthermore, if you're able to take your puppy home and socialize it before it reaches 4 months of age, chances are your Min Pin will do much better in social situations with both other humans and other dogs.

If you buy a Min Pin puppy from a breeder, you will be his first owner, which means he will be a blank slate for you and your love and your training. Puppies are easy to train when they are young, and it's easy to create good habits quickly. In addition, if you purchase a puppy from a reputable breeder, you will often receive lifetime support, whereas with a shelter, there is usually little post-adoption support (if any).

One last consideration in adopting versus buying a Min Pin is cost. Buying a puppy from a breeder can cost anywhere from $1,000 to $6,000, whereas rescuing a dog is usually a fraction of that cost (somewhere between $200 and $500).

Whether you decide to adopt a Min Pin from a shelter, or purchase a puppy from a reputable breeder, you will be lucky to be a Min Pin owner.

Photo Courtesy
of Cheyenne Byers
Coastal Paradise Pinschers

Finding a Reputable Breeder

If you search on the internet for "puppies for sale," or, more specifically, "Min Pins for sale," you will find any number of people selling them. But you don't want to unwittingly buy a puppy from a puppy mill, or from an unskilled breeder who is just trying their hand at breeding. How do you find a breeder that you can trust?

First, find a way to meet the breeder, in person or virtually (if not possible to meet in person because of physical distance or social distancing concerns). Try to get a feel for how he or she interacts with the Min Pins, and vice versa.

Here are some good signs to look for in a breeder:
- The Min Pins are excited to spend time with the breeder.
- The breeder treats the Min Pins with kindness.
- The breeder's house and/or kennel is clean, organized, and free of odors.
- The Min Pins interact well with you and with others, which means they've been well socialized.
- The breeder freely gives you medical history information, proof of health screenings, and is generally knowledgeable about Min Pin health concerns.
- There is a waiting list for puppies.
- The breeder can give you a list of references of people who have already purchased Min Pins from him/her.
- The breeder only produces one or two litters of Min Pin puppies per year.

Likewise, here are some signs that the breeder you're meeting with is not someone you will want to work with:
- The Min Pins shy away from, resist, or act aggressively toward the breeder.
- The breeder uses unkind words or actions toward the Min Pins.
- The breeder's house and/or kennel is dirty, disorganized, or stinks.
- The Min Pins are not sociable with you or with others.
- The breeder does not (or cannot) provide medical history information and proof of health screenings, or does not have any specific information regarding the health of Min Pins.
- The breeder does not provide a list of references of people who have purchased Min Pins from him/her.
- The breeder produces more than two litters of Min Pin puppies per year.

When you're deciding on a breeder, try to meet both parents of the Min Pin. When you're able to meet both dog parents, you can get a good idea of what your Min Pin will be like as an adult dog—both in temperament and in appearance. And ask the breeder to see the parents' official registrations.

Finally, ask as many questions as you can think of about your Min Pin and about the breeder's processes. A puppy is a big investment—of both time and money—and you want to make sure you're taking the time and asking the questions you need to feel at ease about your decision. A good breeder will be patient with you, so don't be afraid to ask too many questions. Likewise, a good breeder will ask you a lot of questions about your home, your family, and your living situation.

Health Tests and Certifications

"If purchasing from a breeder, research them to make sure they are breeding to the breed standard, make sure they are doing structural health testing, not the 'DNA' testing so many people try to pass off as health testing. You want to see test results from the Orthopedic Foundation for Animals (OFA.ORG)."

JACQUELINE SIOTTO-ZWIRN
Sidels Miniature Pinschers

Reputable breeders will be happy to show documentation of health screenings such as OFA (Orthopedic Foundation for Animals) certificates. The OFA's Canine Health Information Center (CHIC) maintains information on the health issues present in specific breeds, as well as providing a protocol for testing dogs. For potential puppy buyers, CHIC certification is a good indicator the breeder takes good health into account when selecting their dogs for breeding.

For Miniature Pinschers, the most common health concern is patellar luxation, when the kneecap (patella) shifts out of its joint because the groove is too narrow. If that happens, the dog may cry out in pain when running or walking. The symptoms come and go, but may require surgery. An OFA evaluation can rule out patellar luxation.

The most serious condition that affects the Miniature Pinscher is a rare disorder known as mucopolysaccharidosis, or MPS VI. It's a genetic defect affecting the way the body processes certain sugar molecules, and a build-up of unprocessed sugar molecules can result in joint deformity, eye cloudiness, and facial deformity. Breeding two carriers can produce affected puppies, so make sure you receive documentation from a breeder who can give you written documentation from the Josephine Deubler Genetic Disease Testing Laboratory at the University of Pennsylvania that your Min Pin's parents were not carriers.

Finally, make sure your breeder gives you evidence of a CAER (The Companion Animal Eye Registry) examination (previously known as the "CERF" examination), an eye exam done only by board-certified veterinary ophthalmologists. The purpose of the CAER exam is to identify any eye problems, and then determine if they are considered inherited in origin.

A good breeder will not hesitate to give you any of these certifications, so make sure you ask.

Breeder Contracts and Guarantees

When you buy your Miniature Pinscher from a breeder, the contract you sign will act not only as a bill of sale, but also as a guarantee of your rights and the seller's rights. It also provides a meaningful history of the generations in your dog's family line.

As with any contract, all terms are completely negotiable, depending on what you and your breeder can come to agreement on. Some items to consider are whether you intend to show your Min Pin, whether you're entitled to breed your dog, and what to do if any health issues arise.

A responsible breeder will be happy to discuss each aspect of your dog's future with you to make sure that the Min Pin is going into a good home. Some of the paperwork when you purchase your puppy may include:

- *Bill of Sale.* The bill of sale (or receipt) is proof that you've paid the breeder for your Min Pin. It will likely contain some clauses required by law, such as a return of your Min Pin and a refund within 48 hours if the dog becomes ill in that time frame. Before you complete the bill of sale for your Min Pin (and pay the breeder), review your state and local municipality laws regarding pet sales.

- *Health Guarantee.* A good breeder will want to keep track of your Min Pin's health and well-being throughout the life of your pup so they can trace any problems in the Min Pin's lineage. Your breeder will likely guarantee good natural health in your Min Pin for at least one or two years. The breeder may ask, in return, that you seek prompt veterinary care for your Min Pin in the case of any health problems, and may require you to keep the breeder apprised of any issues.

- *AKC Registration Application.* A breeder's contract must guarantee that your Miniature Pinscher qualifies for registration with the American

Kennel Club (the AKC). The AKC requires breeders to keep comprehensive records, registering each litter with the AKC, listing the registration of each parent, and keeping track of each member of the new litter. As part of your contract, the breeder should give you a properly completed AKC registration application, which contains the Min Pin's full breeding information: (i) breed, sex and color of the dog; (ii) date of birth; (iii) registered names (and numbers) of the dog's father (sire) and mother (dam); and (iv) the breeder's name. Once you take your Min Pin home, it's up to you to submit the registration with the AKC. If your breeder doesn't produce the required AKC application at the time of sale, you must get a signed statement with all the information listed above to submit to the AKC.

- **Showing Your Min Pin.** If you're planning to take your Miniature Pinscher to compete in dog shows, you will want a guarantee from the breeder that the Min Pin will be fertile and free from hereditary defects. The breeder may put a clause requiring you to show the Min Pin for a set amount of time before you begin breeding him.

- **Reproduction.** Unless you are planning to have your Min Pin compete in dog shows, the breeder could require you to spay or neuter your Min Pin within a certain time frame. Alternatively, the breeder may require you

Photo Courtesy of Barbara Farrell

to spay or neuter the Min Pin if the dog doesn't "exhibit the best standard characteristics of the breed." Or, a breeder may not allow you to breed your Min Pin before he reaches 2 years old, in case health issues arise during that time.

- **Re-homing Your Min Pin.** A good breeder will often require you to notify him if you have to give up your Min Pin for any reason. This allows the breeder to both keep track of the Min Pin throughout his life and to help you place the Min Pin in a trustworthy home. Some breeders will even take the Min Pin themselves if you're not able to care for him. This clause is part of the contract to make sure the Min Pin is well cared for, even if you're unable to do so any longer.

Adopting a Min Pin

"If adopting from a rescue, verify that they are a 501(c) rescue. Understand that the rescue typically has zero back ground on the dog, so proceed with caution, especially if you have other animals and small children at home, and remember to start from scratch in training, as if it was a 12 week old puppy."

JACQUELINE SIOTTO-ZWIRN
Sidels Miniature Pinschers

You've probably heard some version of "adopt, don't shop" when it comes to dogs. It's true: there are many dogs at shelters who don't have homes, and are just looking for their "furever" home.

My Min Pin, Brady, was a rescue dog. He was a senior dog whose owner had passed away. Before I took him home, he'd been living in a foster home for 6 months because no one wanted to deal with all of his issues. For starters, Brady was obese and in need of a major diet overhaul and exercise. He also had bad allergies, which resulted in a lot of hair loss, skin issues, regular trips to the vet, medication, and twice-weekly baths. On top of all of that, he had a congenital dental disease, which meant he was missing a lot of teeth when I adopted him, and had to have 7 other teeth surgically removed under my care. If I had the choice, though, I would adopt Brady again a thousand times over, despite all of the vet bills and baths and special needs that he showed up with.

Why? Because he was my best friend. He showed up in my life at a time when I was thinking of changing careers. I was feeling lost and uncertain and completely alone. And then when he got here, Brady was the love of my life. He was my follow-me-everywhere companion. My "ride or die" bestie. He needed a good home, and I had the means and the time and the attention to give it to him.

What Brady gave me, though, was more than companionship. Even as I write this, nearly three years since he passed away, I just smile when I think of that little guy. Yes, I rescued him and gave him a good home. But what really happened is that Brady rescued me, because he gave my heart a home.

Adopting a dog isn't always the easiest choice, especially when that dog has health or behavioral issues that come with him. But there can be so many benefits to adopting a dog, including the most obvious one: saving that dog from being euthanized.

Photo Courtesy of Alex Meadowcroft

Dogs don't choose to go to shelters. Their owners put them there for some reason or another (allergies, inability to care for the dog, a new baby, a divorce, etc.). Or perhaps, like Brady's owner, they pass away. Or maybe the dog is taken from the owner for mistreatment. Whatever the reason, the dogs aren't there by choice. But if you choose to adopt a Min Pin from a rescue organization, you will be giving that Min Pin the best gift: a loving home.

If you choose to adopt a Min Pin, make sure you talk to the rescue or shelter about the dog and its personality. Many rescue organizations will put their dogs in foster homes, and those foster parents will spend weeks or months caring for the dog you're considering. They'll be a great source of information for you to ask questions about whether the dog is housetrained, how he gets along with other animals and children, what the Min Pin's current schedule is, how energetic he is, etc.

Usually when you adopt a Min Pin, the cost of spay/neuter, first vaccinations, and sometimes even microchipping is included in the adoption price. This can save you some of the upfront costs of adding a new member to your family. Depending on the age of the Min Pin and his prior training, you may also save on housetraining and other training expenses.

Choosing the Perfect Min Pin for You

When you're choosing a Min Pin, you'll want to consider what qualities you're looking for in a dog. If you're searching for a Min Pin that will want endless playtime, socialization, training, and a lot of attention, then go for a puppy. If, instead, you're looking for a dog that's a little more relaxed and already fully trained, then perhaps an older Min Pin from a rescue organization is right for you.

They say, though, that you don't choose a dog. Rather, that dog chooses you. In my own experience, that was certainly the case. For about a week before I met him, I couldn't stop staring at Brady's picture on Petfinder.com. I joked with friends that it was online dating, but for pets. There was something about his little face, and his eyes. I could look at them and just see that he needed me. When I met Brady in person, he was extremely overweight (about 18 pounds). He had balding patches on his skin from a skin allergy condition. He needed dental work. I just knew he needed a good home, and, even more than that, I knew he was my dog. I could just look at him, into those sweet little eyes, and sense what he needed. And, in turn, he followed me around wherever I went—inside or outside. There was already a bond there. The only thing that was missing was the next step: bringing him home.

You can call it intuition, but you'll just know when you meet your Min Pin.

CHAPTER 3

Preparing Your Home for a Miniature Pinscher

"Since Min Pins are notorious escape artists, look for escape routes such as a front door with a screen that doesn't latch, a small nook where they may hide or potty in, missing planks of a fence, or small holes under a fence."

JACQUELINE SIOTTO-ZWIRN
Sidels Miniature Pinschers

Making Your Home Safe for Your Min Pin

How do you make your home safe for a Min Pin? They are clever, high-energy dogs, so you will have to be prepared for their antics. Here are a few tips:

Photo Courtesy
of Olesya Deryabina

- *Make your outdoor space safe for your Min Pin.*

  If you can, create a dedicated outdoor space for your Min Pin to run around and play. However, Min Pins can be incredible escape artists, so it is important that if you have a fenced-in yard, it is safe and secure—no small holes in any fence through which your Min Pin could run off, and the gate must be secure.

- *Make sure all food items are in a cabinet or pantry that your Min Pin cannot access.*

  You can also use child proof latches to keep little Min Pin paws from prying open cabinets. While many food items could be safe to ingest, some of their packaging might not be. Or your Min Pin might go after the things that are dangerous to dogs, such as chocolate, grapes, raisins, etc.—which would end up in a trip to the vet for a stomach pump.

- *Place all medications, cleaners, chemicals, and laundry supplies on high shelves or in cabinets or closets that your Min Pin cannot access.*

- *Keep all trash and recycling bins covered or inside a latched cabinet.*

  Note: if your Min Pin is as crafty as my Brady was, you may have to get creative on how to keep him out of a step-on lidded trash can. There are now pet-proof lidded trash cans, which involve a motion sensor to open the lid; those are probably sufficient to keep your Min Pin out of the trash.

- *Check for and block any small spaces, nooks, or holes inside cabinets or behind washer/dryer units.*

  Min Pins are known for their curiosity, so make sure their curious nature can't lead them into any unsafe places.

- *Put away children's toys, games, or any small items that your Min Pin could potentially eat (or destroy).*

  Likewise, check all the small places where your vacuum cleaner cannot reach, but your Min Pin might, for dangerous items. And move all electrical and phone wires out of reach of chewing.

- *Puppy-proof your garage.*

  In your garage, clean all antifreeze from the floor and driveway, because one taste can be lethal to your Min Pin. And keep all sharp objects and tools out of reach.

Preparing for a new dog is not all that different from preparing for a child. Always assume that your Min Pin will get into trouble, at least for the first few months that you have him and get your training established.

Making Your Home Cozy for Your Min Pin

Miniature Pinschers are small, so any home space is likely big enough for your new Min Pin. But how to make it comfortable enough for your King of Toys?

Buy one or more dog beds. Make sure you invest in one or more dog beds for your Min Pin. Depending on where your dog will sleep at night (in a crate or free to roam), you may want one bed for your living area and one for your bedroom.

Min Pins love to burrow. It's an adorable trait of theirs. Brady used to grab the blanket in his teeth and pull at the blanket with his paws a hundred times, making little grunts and whines along the way as he got his blanket just the way he wanted it. And when it was finally perfect for him, he'd burrow at least his head (if not his whole body) underneath before he collapsed to sleep. Make sure you have at least one blanket for each dog bed, as well as a few in other places in the house where your Min Pin is allowed to be (for example, on the sofa and human beds, if the Min Pin is allowed on them).

Likewise, make sure to put ample bedding and blankets in the dog crate. If you choose to crate-train your Min Pin, make sure there is plenty of bedding and at least one blanket inside the dog crate so he can burrow there, too. A soft padding for the bottom of the crate, and a bigger blanket on top of the padding, should be just perfect.

An exercise pen for your Min Pin could be invaluable and will serve many purposes. You can put it in your yard and allow the Min Pin to hang out in the pen for up to a few hours in a shaded area, temperatures permitting, with your supervision. And since exercise pens are easily collapsible, you could also bring it indoors and use it to allow your Min Pin to hang out indoors without too much supervision. However, a lid is essential, because otherwise your Min Pin will simply jump out of the pen.

Photo Courtesy of Josh Rickett

Stocking Up on Food, Supplies, and Toys

Your first trip to the pet store should be before you bring your Min Pin home. It can be overwhelming to shop for a new dog, but here is a list of essentials to help you with your transition:

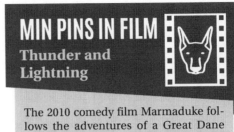

MIN PINS IN FILM
Thunder and Lightning

The 2010 comedy film Marmaduke follows the adventures of a Great Dane named *Marmaduke*. The movie features two Miniature Pinschers named Thunder and Lighting, voiced by Damon Wayans, Jr. and Marlon Wayans, respectively.

- *Collar and/or harness*
  Miniature Pinschers have tiny necks, which makes finding collars that fit (or that they can't slip out of) challenging. Another issue with small dogs with collars is that they can unwittingly strain their neck and trachea by pulling on the leash (which is potentially life threatening). That's why harnesses work better for walking Min Pins, although you can certainly still use a collar to hold his ID tag. A no-pull harness (i.e., a front lead harness) can work to deter your Min Pin from pulling on a leash and train him to stop this behavior. It will have a front-clip option for the leash, which will slow his momentum and divert his movements to the side.

- *ID tag*
  Get an ID tag made with your Min Pin's name and your phone number in case your Min Pin ever gets lost. Attach it to his collar or his harness.

- *Leash*
  A standard nylon or leather leash will be the best option for your Min Pin. You may want to start with a shorter leash (4 feet), then have a longer one for when your Min Pin does better on a leash. I don't recommend retractable leashes, especially for new puppies. They are less reliable and offer you less control over your Min Pin.

- *Dog food*
  Providing your Min Pin with proper nutrition is extremely important. Ask your breeder and/or veterinarian for recommendations on what brand and type of food your Min Pin should eat.

- *Food and water bowls.*
  Bowls can be made of ceramic, plastic, or stainless steel

- *Crate*
  It's up to you whether you decide to crate-train your Min Pin, and we'll talk about that in Chapter 8. If you do get one, it should be large enough

for your Min Pin to sit, turn around, and lie down comfortably, but not much bigger than that.

- **Bedding**
  Dog beds, blankets, and towels are all useful tools for making your Min Pin comfortable in his new home.

- **Treats**
  Treats are great for training and for giving positive reinforcement for the behaviors you want him to continue. Make sure treats are easy to chew and healthy. Ask your veterinarian or breeder for recommendations.

- **Toys**
  All dogs (especially puppies) need toys and lots of them to focus their need for chewing on something appropriate (i.e., not your furniture or your shoes). Your Min Pin's toys should be durable and made with puppy-safe materials that can't be destroyed. Always supervise your Min Pin with toys to make sure he doesn't eat small pieces. You can also get interactive puzzle toys to help stimulate your Min Pin's brain and keep him busy longer.

- **Bathing and grooming items**
  Your Min Pin's shiny coat won't need too many baths, but if he's like most puppies, he will get dirty often. Have some puppy-safe shampoo around just in case. You should also have a dog brush and nail clippers.

Preparing Children and Current Pets

Before you bring your Min Pin home, make sure you do a test run at the breeder's home or the rescue organization where your kids can meet the Min Pin, and vice versa.

If that initial meeting goes well, then you can start to prepare your children for your Min Pin's arrival at home by teaching them how to gently touch and pet the dog. Kids love animals, but they don't usually realize when they are squeezing or pulling a dog's coat. Teach your kids instead to pet your Min Pin with slow, gentle movements. You can have them practice on a stuffed animal before you bring the Min Pin home.

Also, teach your children to approach your Min Pin slowly, from the side, and have them stop with enough room to allow the dog to come to the child. Having your child approach your Min Pin in a calm fashion with enough space will give the Min Pin the ability to watch the child without getting overwhelmed.

It's also essential that you prepare your children for the warning signs or red flags that your Min Pin may not want to interact with them. Some red flags to teach them include growls, walking away from the child, resisting being held, retreating to a space where the child cannot get to the dog, etc. In addition, kids (and adults alike) should be on the lookout for body language from the dog. If you notice your Min Pin's tail is rigid, his ears are back, or the fur on his back is raised, then your kids should give the Min Pin some space. He is telling you he's not sure if he is ready to greet you.

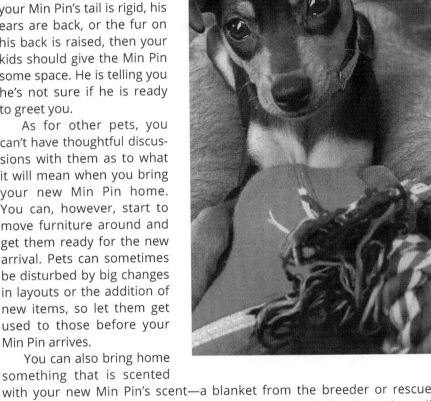

Photo Courtesy of Brian Strumwasser

As for other pets, you can't have thoughtful discussions with them as to what it will mean when you bring your new Min Pin home. You can, however, start to move furniture around and get them ready for the new arrival. Pets can sometimes be disturbed by big changes in layouts or the addition of new items, so let them get used to those before your Min Pin arrives.

You can also bring home something that is scented with your new Min Pin's scent—a blanket from the breeder or rescue. Allowing your pets to get used to your Min Pin's scent before he arrives will make his arrival less of a surprise.

It's also helpful to have baby gates installed to give your other pets a place to retreat from their new housemate. You can install them at the bottom or top of stairways to block off entire floors, or between rooms. Installing these in advance will not only give them time to get used to the new gates, but it will be handy to have them around so separation can be done easily when your new Min Pin arrives. If you have cats, tall cat houses or trees make for an excellent escape destination that your Min Pin won't be able to reach.

Photo Courtesy
of Alesha Snyder

Preparing an Outdoor Space for Your Min Pin

While Min Pins are tiny creatures, they have endless amounts of energy and curiosity, so having a dedicated outdoor space for your Min Pin to run around and play will save you a lot of effort.

Because Min Pins are so curious and intelligent, however, they can be incredible escape artists, so it is important that if you have a fenced-in yard, it is safe and secure. This means that the fence cannot have any small holes through which your Min Pin could run off, and the gate must be secure. Min Pins also have a tendency to dig, so you'll have to make sure your fence goes all the way to the ground. If it doesn't, you can use chicken wire, hardware cloth, or a piece of chain-link fence and attach it to the base of the fence. (You can bury it, or lay it on top of the grass and hold it down with rocks, gravel, mulch, or anything heavy your Min Pin won't be able to move.)

If you don't have a fence, just make sure that you take your Min Pin out on a harness and leash at all times. Alternatively, you can also install a cable dog run that attaches like a leash but gives your Min Pin a little more freedom to roam about the yard. Also, comb the yard for and remove small, foreign objects, and replace any loose slats or boards.

And start to scope out some good neighborhood walks for you and your Min Pin. This King of Toys will also enjoy being the King of the Neighborhood, so take a few walks around the blocks to see what areas are safe, and whether there are parks or green spaces nearby where your new best friend can roam around. You may even luck out and have a fenced-in dog park nearby.

Choosing a Veterinarian for Your Min Pin

If you adopted your Min Pin from a breeder, you may have already been given a list of veterinarians that the breeder prefers. If that's not the case, however, you'll have to do your own research on which veterinarian to choose to work with your Min Pin. While the internet is a great source of information, and you'll want to do your homework, start by asking friends, family members, and neighbors about their experiences with local veterinarians.

Try to see the vet facility before you take your Min Pin there. Take a look around and note whether the place is clean, up-to-date, and organized. Also, ask about how many vets are on their staff. A lot of vet practices share patients, so you'll want to make sure they have enough people to cover for your main veterinarian should he/she take a vacation. Talk to the staff (and, if you're able, the vet) and ask questions. Most good veterinarian practices will have a pamphlet, handout, or plenty of advice about bringing a new puppy home.

Photo Courtesy
of Ian Birch

Also, consider the cost and location of the veterinarian practice. In the case of an emergency, you'll want your vet office to be as close to your home as possible, at most an hour away. And ask about prices. Some vets charge more than others, so check to see if their prices fit into your budget before you commit.

Make sure to set up your vet appointment to occur within a few days of bringing your Min Pin home. Breeders generally require a vet visit within three days of bringing the dog home, and also require yearly physicals and necessary vaccinations as a condition of sale. If you get your Min Pin from a rescue or shelter, an immediate exam is even more important, because the dogs have unknown backgrounds and might have been exposed to contagious diseases.

CHAPTER 4

Bringing Home Your Miniature Pinscher

Picking Up Your Min Pin

Getting ready to pick up your new Min Pin is such an exciting time. The car ride home is where it might sink in: you're officially a new Min Pin dog mom or dog dad! When you pick up your Min Pin at the breeder's or the shelter, you'll want to bring along some treats, something to chew (like a bully stick), a blanket or towel, the leash and harness, and poop bags and cleaning supplies (in case your new Min Pin has an accident in the

Photo Courtesy of Cynthia and Arthur Diaz

car). And a crate, if you're traveling on your own. Before you get in your car, make sure you harness and leash your Min Pin and take him on a quick walk so he can relieve himself one last time.

If you can, bring someone with you to help supervise and keep your Min Pin occupied (otherwise, he will want to investigate every inch of your car). Have your passenger

CELEBRITY MIN PIN
Herman the Min Pin ★★★★

The most popular Min Pin on social media is probably Herman Collett. With over fifteen thousand followers on Instagram (@herman.the.minpin), Herman and his sister Dobby offer a weekly dose of cuteness to their followers on the social media platform.

hang out in the backseat with the Min Pin so he doesn't distract you while you're driving. Your passenger can hold your Min Pin in a blanket, or you can put your Min Pin on a blanket on the seat, but make sure the passenger securely holds him so he's safe during the car ride. To keep him occupied, you can give your Min Pin something to chew, like a bully stick or a rawhide.

If you can't bring anyone else along, you can put your Min Pin in a crate. Place the crate in a flat, safe place (like the backseat), and secure it in place with a seatbelt. Make sure the crate has plenty of treats, a blanket or towel, and something to chew inside to keep your Min Pin occupied on his first car ride home.

You'll want to make your Min Pin's first car ride as fun and comfortable as possible so he'll be okay with other car rides in the future. Barking or crying is totally normal, so do your best to try not to react. (If you get excited or anxious, your Min Pin will pick up on it and become more fearful.) Just try to be as calm and easygoing as possible to reassure your Min Pin that everything is okay.

Bringing Your Min Pin Home

Congratulations! You're now a proud dog parent to a Miniature Pinscher, one of the proudest dogs. When you bring your Min Pin home, make sure to let him walk around your house or neighborhood before you bring him inside. That way, he can relieve himself outdoors (instead of inside the house).

When you walk inside, show your Min Pin his water bowl, so he knows where he can always get water. Depending on whether you have kids or other pets, decide whether you want to keep your Min Pin on a leash for the first few hours that he's at home with you, or whether you let him roam freely.

Photo Courtesy of Timothy Fendley

If you choose the latter option, make sure you keep an eye on him. Not only will his curious personality take over and he'll want to explore every nook and cranny of your house, but he may also be inclined to relieve himself indoors if you don't keep a good watch. Dogs (especially male dogs) love to mark their territory, so if you see any signs that your Min Pin wants to mark, grab him and take him outside to do his business.

Give your Min Pin the grand tour of all the rooms and places he can access. Bringing a dog home can be a little nerve-wracking for both of you; the best way to handle it is to stay calm so your Min Pin can take your lead. He will want to sniff and inspect everything, so let him. It's his time to get comfortable with all the new smells, sounds, and surroundings.

Make sure to show the dog all the stuff you bought to make him comfortable, like his bed, his blankets, and all of his new toys. Your Min Pin may relax right away, but it may take some time for him to acclimate to his new surroundings.

Introducing Your Min Pin to Your Children

You've had the talks about approaching slowly, gentle touching, and what warning signs to look for if a dog doesn't want to be touched/followed/held. But now you're really bringing your Min Pin home. How do you get your kids and your Min Pin on board with this new family dynamic?

Take it slowly. Have your kids avoid wild movements or loud sounds. Most kids want to hug and squeeze dogs right away, but they need to stay calm. Sudden body movements can easily frighten your Min Pin (or any dog) and cause them to protect themselves by biting or nipping.

Keep your Min Pin on a leash to start the introductions. Have your children toss training treats to the Min Pin from a short distance so he starts to trust them. When he realizes that your children are, in fact, treat factories, he should warm up pretty quickly. Let your Min Pin guide you. If, while on leash, he acts as though he's ready to approach them, give him a little more slack and let him say hi.

Before letting your kids pet your Min Pin, let the dog sniff each child. Dogs use their sense of smell to say hello and find out who you are. Have the children stand still, allowing the dog to sniff around them, and be careful about offering hands to smell. Have your kids tuck in their fingers, allow your Min Pin to sniff the backside of their hands, and avoid pushing hands

Photo Courtesy
of Caroline Canlas

into the dog's face. As an added caution, make sure your kids NEVER bend over the dog's face, in case he decides he's not sure about them and reacts.

If your Min Pin isn't giving any warning signs, and he's acting as though he'd love some affection, then let your kids pet his back or his sides. The face or the head is a more vulnerable place for dogs, so save ear and chin scratches for when your kids and your Min Pin are best friends.

If all goes well on the leash, and your Min Pin relaxes around your kids— meaning, no warning signs like growling, back hairs standing, barking, baring teeth, etc.—and willingly gets close to them without any negative reaction, then perhaps it's time to take him off his leash.

Let your Min Pin run around and visit with your kids, but just make sure you are there to supervise and step in if necessary in case anything goes awry. If he's a puppy from a breeder, he will likely do just fine. If you've rescued him, whether as a puppy or as an adult, you'll need a bit more caution. You never know what a rescue pup has been through, or what his triggers might be.

Photo Courtesy
of Jessica Woolcott

As time goes on, your kids and your Min Pin will likely reach a good level of comfort with each other, but never leave a small child and a dog unsupervised, no matter how much you trust that dog. To protect your kids and your Min Pin, it's best to always be nearby and watch them interact together.

Introducing Your Min Pin to Your Other Pets

When first introducing your Min Pin to other dogs in the home, use a sturdy baby gate to separate them. Start to notice how they interact through the gate, and reward positive interactions by giving treats to the dogs.

When the dogs act as though they want to spend time together, give them trial runs in the same room without the baby gate. But make sure that there are no toys, foods, treats, etc., around the house that the Min Pin and your other dogs could become territorial over. And be cautious of situations that could lead to conflict, like becoming overly excited. Closely monitor the dogs when they are together, rewarding them with treats, until you are 100% confident they are comfortable and safe with each other.

My Min Pin, Brady, wasn't keen on other dogs. (I suspect he didn't have good socialization when he was a puppy.) He wasn't bothered by them, but he wasn't a fan of playing with other dogs, whether at doggy day care, the dog park, or with friends' and family members' dogs. But for a couple of months, we stayed at my parents' house, where they also had a dog, Bella. Brady and Bella never became the best of friends, but they coexisted fairly peacefully. We had to keep them separate at mealtimes (lest one would try to eat the other's food), but otherwise, they got along fine, mostly because Brady established his dominance over Bella (a dog twice his size) as the alpha.

For introducing your Min Pin to your cat, allow your cat to have its own special place where only she can escape. Perhaps it's a single floor reserved for your cat, barred off with a baby gate. Or maybe it's a section of your main living floor. Whatever it is, make sure your cat has some of its own space to start. You may find that for the first while that your Min Pin lives with you, your cat may hide somewhere the Min Pin can't reach her. That's normal. Cats take a little longer to adjust to new roommates than dogs do.

When your Min Pin is around your cat, make sure you keep an eye on the interactions. Discourage your Min Pin from being too rough with your cat. Even though your Min Pin may only be the size of your cat (maybe smaller!), he is likely much stronger than any cat and could cause damage. Over time, they will likely learn how to play very well together.

For help with introductions that don't seem to be going well, you can always contact a professional trainer or animal behaviorist.

Photo Courtesy
of Shivali Amin

The First Night at Home

You've survived your first day with your Min Pin, and hopefully all has gone well. No bad interactions with current family members or pets, no (or minimal) accidents indoors, and (fingers crossed) your Min Pin has started to relax in his new home.

Nighttime might bring a different set of challenges. On Brady's first night at home, he got very anxious. I had set him up to sleep in his dog bed, with plenty of blankets for burrowing. At the time, I lived in a one-bedroom apartment in Manhattan, so he certainly knew his way around the place; it wasn't big enough for him to get lost. I went in with the resolve that he would, under no circumstances, sleep in my bed, despite the fact that his foster mom had let him sleep in hers. He had his bed, I had mine. Or so I thought.

When I went into the bedroom and turned out the lights, Brady came right by my side and whined and cried. I showed him his bed again, and returned to mine. He came in whining a few more times. I ignored him again. At some point, we both were able to get to sleep. In the morning, however, I awoke to a large puddle of urine. Either Brady was so anxious that he forgot he wasn't supposed to pee inside, or he was doing it to spite me for making him sleep away from me.

After that, I totally caved. The next night, I let him sleep in my bed. And it was smooth sailing. No more whining, no more crying, and not once during the five and a half years that he lived with me did he go to the bathroom in the house at night.

Whether you let your Min Pin sleep with you is your choice. But the lesson is this: if your Min Pin is crying in the middle of the night on the first night that you have him at home, take him outside, just in case he's telling you that he needs to relieve himself one last time. And if your Min Pin is a puppy, you may have to get up once or twice a night regardless to help with his housetraining. (We'll cover housetraining in Chapter 5.)

And then wake up the next morning, and be prepared to start all over again with all of it!

Your Min Pin's First Vet Visit

At your Min Pin's first vet visit, the vet will weigh your Min Pin; listen to his heart and lungs; take his temperature; examine his skin and coat; examine his eyes, ears, nose, teeth, mouth, and genitalia; examine his feces (most vets will require you to bring a sample along); palpate his lymph nodes and abdomen; and discuss any questions you might have about medications, vaccinations, dental care, breed-related issues, microchipping, spaying/neutering, and taking care of your dog at home. (Make sure you bring along any important paperwork from the breeder or the rescue about prior medical care, vaccinations, microchipping, etc.)

Your Min Pin may be frightened at the vet's office, especially if it's his first vet visit, or he's a rescue. Being at the vet gave Brady anxiety. He would shake in my arms, whine, pace, and shed a lot of his fur. Just walking into the building made him freak out. If that's the case for your Min Pin, hold him if he needs you to, and let him know everything will be okay. Most dogs will forget about the vet the minute you get home, but the time that you're there can be stressful for your dog and for you. Take a few deep breaths and stay calm for your Min Pin.

Photo Courtesy
of Kyle Patrick Scanlon

Puppy Classes

Chances are, you've seen signs at your local pet store or vet's office for puppy classes and wondered, are these right for my Min Pin? Enrolling your Min Pin in a puppy obedience training class is an ideal opportunity for you and your dog to bond. Min Pins are alpha dogs, which means they will be the boss of you if you're not careful, so creating a strong bond where your Min Pin knows that you are his leader is essential. A puppy obedience class will not only help you train your Min Pin, but it will also help to train you to become the strong, positive leader your Min Pin deserves. Being the leader in your dog's life will help to ensure he follows the rules you have established, and once your Min Pin knows you are his leader, you will have his never-ending loyalty and respect.

Photo Courtesy of Hailey Baldwin

Another advantage to enrolling your Min Pin in puppy obedience training classes is socialization. Exposing puppies to other dogs (and humans) early in their life is crucial for creating positive social experiences. Your Min Pin will get a chance to socialize with a variety of other dog breeds, and can learn how to play and get along with other dogs. And because other dog owners will participate in these classes, your Min Pin will get to socialize with other people, too.

In your puppy classes, your Min Pin will also learn basic commands such as "sit" and "stay," as well as how to walk properly on a leash. The trainers will also offer dog training tips to help make training your Min Pin easier.

CHAPTER 5
Housetraining Your Miniature Pinscher

"Min Pins can be very stubborn. This can make house training more difficult, even taking longer than other breeds sometimes. Consistency is key, pick a potty training schedule and stick to it."

KAREN MERICA
Lilbears Kennels

Photo Courtesy
of Cheyenne Byers
Coastal Paradise Pinschers

Options for Potty Training Your Dog

Potty training your Min Pin is a task that will require a lot of effort, consistency, watchfulness, and discipline, but one that is worth it if you do it well. There are a lot of options for potty training your Min Pin, including using a consistent (and frequent) walk schedule, indoor potty training tools like puppy pads, rewarding positive behavior, crate training, pet gates and playpens, and relying on pet sitters and dog walkers to help when you're away from the house.

FUN FACT

How Popular Are They?

According to the American Kennel Club, Miniature Pinschers were the 74th most popular breed in America in 2020. In 2013, Min Pins were ranked as the 53rd most popular breed in America.

Using a Consistent Walk Schedule

Setting up a consistent walk schedule will be one of the most helpful tools you can use as a dog owner to get your Min Pin to relieve himself outdoors (instead of on your favorite carpet or piece of furniture). The age of your dog will have an impact on how often you have to take your Min Pin out. If he's a puppy, you may want to take your Min Pin out every two hours as both of you begin to investigate how often he needs to go. Puppies have tiny bladders, and any time they eat or drink, they will likely need to go. The same is true for solid foods and solid waste.

A typical adult Min Pin may be able to wait 6-8 hours between walks, depending on the schedule you establish for him. But you should consider starting with 4-hour increments, and working up to the longer periods the more the two of you get to know each other and your routine together.

When you're setting up a schedule for your Min Pin, monitor your Min Pin's habits and daily events and see what works best for both of you. With a young Min Pin, you should expect to take the puppy out at least every two hours, and especially at these times:

1. First thing in the morning, before you give him his first meal;
2. After your Min Pin eats or drinks (set up a food schedule, Chapter 9);
3. After coming out of the crate or after spending time alone;
4. After chewing a toy or bone, or playing indoors;
5. Just before bedtime.

Photo Courtesy of Nicole Gray

This list (and the idea of walks every two hours) probably seems intimidating, but if you work with your Min Pin to let him know that outside is the place to go and you will take him as often as he needs you to, he will quickly begin to understand. Remember: he's one of the smartest breeds around! You'll also need to watch your Min Pin carefully for signs that he needs to relieve himself. Some puppies whine, some bark, and others scratch at the door. Whatever the signal your Min Pin gives, you'll become attuned to it over time. Just keep your eye on him, and let him lead you.

My Min Pin, Brady, was a whiner. If he was excited, he whined. If he was nervous, he whined. If he wanted a treat, he whined. If he had to go to the bathroom, he whined. When I first got him, I had him on a walk schedule that his foster mom had passed along: 4 times per day. And because he was an adult dog, four walks were more than enough for him potty-wise, except for the days when he'd had his baths. Brady was a funny little character. He loved running water of any kind: hoses, fountains, sinks, bathtub faucets, you name it. During bath time, Brady would stare and whine and bark and play with the water running out of the faucet, drinking as much of it as he could while I scrubbed and cleaned his coat. Then he'd come out, dry off, and we'd go back to our lives (or so I thought). I noticed that he would always whine after his bath; initially, I thought he was just asking for more playtime with the faucet. Eventually, after a few accidents, I began to interpret those whines—he had ingested so much water during his bath that he inevitably had to go to the bathroom within 30 minutes. The more time you spend with your Min Pin, the easier it will be to attune yourself to his wants and needs (eccentric as they may be), and the better your housetraining routine will go.

Indoor Elimination Options

Puppy pads and paper training can be a tricky option. While it's handy to have an indoor option for rainy days or days when you have to be out of the house for longer periods without help, this can prolong the process of housetraining and may also teach your Min Pin that going to the bathroom indoors is acceptable, long after you've tried to retire the puppy pads.

If you plan to paper-train your Min Pin, confine him to an area with enough room for a space to sleep, a space to play, and a separate place to eliminate. In the designated elimination area, use several layers of newspaper or puppy pads (found at any pet store). You can also get specialized relief areas that look like grass, so it's more like the outdoors. Once your Min Pin matures and needs less time between walks, you can work up to outdoor elimination all of the time.

Rewarding Positive Behavior

Many trainers and vets encourage using "fear-free" tactics and "positive reinforcement training" because it's shown that the less afraid your dog is in any situation, the better it will be for him. Makes sense, right? If you, as a human,

Photo Courtesy of Alesha Snyder

*Photo Courtesy
of Ebru Tunc*

are learning something new, would you do better with someone yelling at you every time you do it wrong, or encouraging you when you are able to do it well?

That's why rewarding positive behavior works so well with potty training your Min Pin. Not only does it make training an enjoyable (and hopefully stress-free experience for your Min Pin), but it also helps you to build trust with your Min Pin over time. By rewarding positive behavior, you can help your Min Pin find a sense of pride in exhibiting good behavior, and it will create a bond between your Min Pin and you so you feel like a team.

You can start by actively watching for positive behaviors that your Min Pin already does (like relieving himself outdoors), and let him know that you approve with some praise and a little treat. When you create that association between your Min Pin doing the right thing and you approving and showing affection with treats, your Min Pin will look to find other ways to work with you and win your admiration.

When using positive reinforcement for housetraining, the easiest thing to do is to gently encourage your dog to go outside. Pay attention when you're walking your Min Pin, and when he does relieve himself outside, reward him with praise ("good boy!") and a small training treat. With consistency, your Min Pin will start to understand that going to the bathroom outside will lead him to get treats and praise, two things he would love from his pack leader (you!).

But here's what you need to know: mistakes will happen. Your Min Pin will undoubtedly have a few accidents in your house. Prepare yourself for it, expect it to happen, and then when it does, you can be prepared. First, make a startling noise if you catch your Min Pin in the act, and immediately take him outside. Reward positive behavior by giving your Min Pin a treat if he finishes what he started outside. Then, come in and clean the spot he used immediately and thoroughly so he's not tempted to mark there again.

Don't punish your Min Pin for relieving himself indoors. At some point, you may have been around someone rubbing a dog's nose in their accident and saying "bad dog." This doesn't fix the problem; it might only make him afraid of going to the bathroom in front of you, in general, and might cause him to sneak off and find a private elimination spot of his own. Instead, just clean it up. Make sure you clean the affected area as thoroughly as you can to get rid of any scent—once a puppy has marked his scent in an area, he will be more likely to continue to mark on that spot.

It's a simple idea, really: with positive reinforcement, your Min Pin starts to realize that if he goes to the bathroom outside, he gets a treat and praise. If he goes to the bathroom inside, no reward and no praise. Because your Min Pin is incredibly intelligent, positive rewards will persuade him to relieve himself outside.

*Photo Courtesy
of Hailey Baldwin*

Crate Training

"Crate training is the best! Put them out after every nap and praise them like crazy when they do potty outside. If you are napping and the puppy wakes up, don't play with it--physically take it outside and use your word for potty. Once the puppy has done this make a big deal about what a good job they did and reward them with a treat. I use Cheerios: it's a low fat, low sugar, healthy treat."

JACQUELINE SIOTTO-ZWIRN
Sidels Miniature Pinschers

Some people are against crates for their dogs. But the idea behind them makes a lot of sense: dogs are den creatures who feel comfortable in small spaces. The reason crates can help for housetraining is because dogs are clean animals, and they don't want to lie around on a urine-soaked blanket. The most important part of using a crate for housetraining is making sure your crate is the right size for your Min Pin. It should be large enough that he can sit, turn around, and lie down, but no bigger. Any extra room will invite your Min Pin to use the spare space for eliminating. Many crates come with partitions so you can adjust the size as your Min Pin grows.

A crate may be a great nighttime option for potty training your Min Pin, and may save you a lot of trips to the yard in your pajamas. Just make sure you take your Min Pin outside to eliminate immediately before crating him and immediately after you take him out of the crate.

Note, however, that while an older Min Pin might do well in a crate for 6-8 hours, a young Min Pin puppy might not be capable of holding his pee or poop for that long. This could result in a huge mess to clean up—the crate, your Min Pin, and any paw prints that he makes on the floor on the way out. And having your Min Pin lying in the same spot as his pee and poop will interfere with his natural instinct not to relieve himself where he sleeps. This could result in setbacks in the potty training process, so just keep an ear out for your Min Pin when he's crated. If he's whining, crying, or scratching, it's time to let him out of the crate and take him outside.

Doggy Gates and Playpens

When you are potty training your Min Pin, supervision is a must. However, it's often hard to keep track of a puppy who likes to explore every room of the house (especially a curious, intelligent puppy like your Min Pin). This is why a movable pet gate or an exercise pen will work wonders to manage your Min Pin's new environment. Just set up the gate or the exercise pen to confine your Min Pin to a space you can easily watch. For example, let's say you're cooking a big meal but don't want your Min Pin underfoot or far away where you can't see him. Find a space in or near the kitchen that is out of the way and easy to clean where you can set up your Min Pin's play area. Also, although Min Pins are tiny creatures, they are able to jump higher than you think, so make sure your movable gate is high enough that he can't clear it (a standard 30-inch gate should be tall enough), or if you have an exercise pen, make sure it has a lid.

Let him know you're watching him in his shrunken living space. Make sure he's got plenty of toys or chews to entertain himself, and every so often, look at him and say "good boy!" when he's not getting into trouble. If you can catch him needing to use the bathroom—sniffing, pacing, scratching, and whining are all good signs—quickly take him outside. You can also give him a separate space within his pen or his gated area that he can use as a bathroom—puppy pads, newspapers, etc.—in case you're too occupied to watch his every move. If you don't catch your Min Pin in time, no stress. That's why you've confined him to an area that's easy to clean!

Leaving Your Dog Home Alone

Leaving your Min Pin home alone for the first time can be stressful, both for you and your Min Pin. Maybe you need to go to the store for a quick errand; maybe you need to go to work for a whole day. Whichever is the case, you need to make sure that your Min Pin feels safe, loved, and has plenty of entertainment (as well as a bathroom plan for your absence).

First, make sure you have set up a safe area for your Min Pin. Maybe it's his crate, if it's a shorter period of time. You can lure him in there with treats, tell him "good boy" when he gets in and settles down, and be on your way. But make sure you take him outside the moment you arrive home, whether it's been 30 minutes or 4 hours.

If you're going to be away longer than your Min Pin can comfortably hold it, you can set up a bigger confinement area. It should be easy to clean (think linoleum or tile floors) and have nothing of value that he could ingest or destroy by chewing, digging, or relieving himself. Make sure it has somewhere for him to lie down (a dog bed, a blanket, etc.) as well as a play area, complete with toys and chews. Your Min Pin will be happiest if he has something constructive to do when he's confined; it will make him feel like he has purpose and help him feel happier when you're not around. Toys like Kongs (stuffed with dog food, treats, peanut butter, etc.) are great for alone activities because the food that comes out of the toy will reinforce his chewing on the Kong (instead of on your furniture). Finally, make sure he has a spot where he can relieve himself if you don't have any help.

If you have to work long hours and are unable to spend much time at home with your Min Pin, consider finding a puppy sitter who can help you on long days away from home. A professional pet sitter, a neighbor, or a friend could help with potty training and outdoor potty breaks while you're away. That person could also just spend time at home with your Min Pin while he's in his confinement area—that way, your Min Pin gets used to days without you, and still has some time to himself.

When your Min Pin seems like you can leave him for longer periods, a dog walker is a great solution. When I first adopted Brady I worked long hours 5 days a week. I lived near a doggy day care facility that had great reviews, and I set him up for two days a week at daycare so he could socialize with other dogs, and three days a week at home with two walks with a professional dog walker per day. It was expensive, but it was totally worth it. Not only was Brady fully cared for during those days, but he also formed a forever bond with his main dog walker. She fell in love with him, just as I had, and she became my trusted, go-to person to watch him when I left town to travel. Brady felt loved and attended to, even when I wasn't the person taking care of him, and I never had to worry about accidents while I was at work.

CHAPTER 6
Socializing with People and Animals

The Importance of Good Socialization

During your Min Pin's first few months of life, he will be exposed to a variety of experiences that will permanently shape his personality and how he will react to different situations as an adult. Before a dog reaches 16 weeks of age, this is a critical, formative period, during which positive experiences of the world around your Min Pin will help him adjust to situations for the rest of his life. To properly socialize your Min Pin, you'll want to gently expose him to a wide variety of people, places, and situations so he is okay with sights, sounds, and smells of all kinds. It will help your Min Pin be free of fear of other dogs, children, and maybe even trips to the vet.

Photo Courtesy of Alex Meadowcroft

Photo Courtesy
of Cheyenne Byers
Coastal Paradise Pinschers

My Min Pin was far from well-socialized by the time I adopted him at the age of 7. Brady was great with a lot of things, like meeting new (adult) people, spending time in places he'd never been, exploring all sorts of terrains on hikes and walks, and staying with his favorite humans when I needed to be away. He did not do particularly well, however, with children, including my young nieces. I had to keep him leashed or separated in another room if there were ever kids in our apartment, just in case he decided he wanted to bark, growl, or lunge at them. He also wasn't great with other dogs if he didn't know them well: he would react with fear-based aggression if they approached his face. He got frightened at the sight of canes and walkers, which made me wonder if he'd been abused by his former owner (an elderly person). He panicked at the sound of thunder. He shook with fear and anxiety the moment we neared the veterinarian's office. And so on and so forth. He was the perfect companion for me, a single woman who lived alone at the time, but he certainly wouldn't have been okay in a family with small children or other dogs.

This is why it's so important to socialize your Min Pin early, and expose him to as many situations as safe and possible. Keep in mind, as you socialize your Min Pin, you'll want to keep a close eye on his reaction to whatever situation you expose him to so that you can step in and take him out of the situation if your Min Pin seems at all frightened. And always follow up a socialization session with lots of praise, petting, treats, and love.

Photo Courtesy of Annie Hughes

Socializing with Other Dogs

"Do not carry the Min Pin when practicing socializing. Do all introductions on neutral territory and on a leash so you have control. If the Min Pin responds to a new dog by barking, correct them immediately, especially if it's a bigger dog. DO NOT laugh at how funny it is that a little dog is barking at the big dog--that encourages the behavior and you will have issues down the road."

JACQUELINE SIOTTO-ZWIRN
Sidels Miniature Pinschers

If you've gotten your Min Pin from a reputable breeder, the socialization process with other dogs would have started there. To continue that process, or to start if you didn't get your Min Pin from a breeder, you can enroll him in puppy classes. Puppies as young as eight weeks old can meet other dogs and people in a controlled, safe environment supervised by a trainer. A good class will require your Min Pin to have at least one vaccine, and they will disinfect the space before puppies gather to lower the risk of contagious disease. These classes will help your Min Pin understand basic commands, and will also expose your Min Pin to other dogs and people.

You can also arrange playdates with other dogs. If you have a friend with a puppy or friendly adult dog, you can set up a playdate at your home or theirs. This is a good way for your Min Pin to get to know other dogs in a safe and low-key way. Make sure you ask your friend about his/her dog's aggression level, what its triggers are, etc., so you know in advance whether that dog will be a good fit for your Min Pin. And when they do meet, you can always use a pet gate to separate them until they get comfortable with one another.

Dog parks are also a great place for socialization, but they're less controlled than puppy classes or prearranged meetings. Because you never know what diseases other dogs at the park could be carrying, you'll want to make sure your Min Pin is at least 4 months of age and fully vaccinated for at least 10 days before you take him to a dog park. Likewise, if your Min Pin is showing any signs of illness or contagious disease, don't bring him to the park (hopefully, other owners will follow this same etiquette). As for socializing with other dogs at the park, keep an eye on your Min Pin. If he's showing any signs of discomfort or aggression, remove him from those situations. You also never know what behavior is typical of the dogs that show up at the dog parks, or how their owners will handle it, so just watch every interaction with caution, and be prepared to scoop up your Min Pin and head home if things do not go as planned.

Photo Courtesy
of Maria Björn

Meeting New People

When you have a dog, especially one as handsome, compact, and regal as a Min Pin, you will have people flocking to meet you and your pup anywhere you go. This is great for socializing your Min Pin, because the more people he's exposed to during his first few months of life, the more comfortable he'll be when he meets new people for his whole life.

There are plenty of ways for your Min Pin to make new human friends. Because he's small, portable, and easy to handle, you can take him to pet-friendly stores very easily. He can sit in the cart or walk proudly beside you, and everyone will be so excited to meet your King of Toys. Home improvement stores, especially on weekdays, are a great place for your Min Pin to meet a lot of people of all sizes, genders, and races. Pet stores are also full of various folks, and they tend to have dogs, too, so you can work on socializing with people and dogs at the same time. You could also sit at the entrance outside of a shopping mall, and have the people going in and out give your Min Pin treats so he's rewarded for dealing with a high-traffic visitation area.

In addition to pet-friendly stores and malls, you can take your Min Pin on car rides through different neighborhoods, on country drives, and maybe even through a few drive-throughs so he gets to meet people in the windows. Starbucks, for example, is great with dogs. If you ask for a "pup-o-chino" along with your human order, they'll give you a small free cup of whipped cream for your Min Pin. Is it a healthy snack that he should have every day? Certainly not. But it's a great once-in-a-while treat, and it also gives your Min Pin the sense that the people who work in drive-throughs are not a threat.

Parks (other than dog parks) are also a wonderful place to let your dog exercise, explore the outdoors, and meet new folks. Brady and I used to go for a long walk, set up a blanket in Riverside Park or Central Park, and let people come to meet us as they were interested. A note for letting strangers meet your Min Pin—carrying extra training treats for them to give your Min Pin is always a great idea. Your Min Pin will start to see that letting strangers be friendly with him will earn him some rewards and praise, and positive associations will form.

FUN FACT
Ace Underwood

American singer, songwriter, and record producer Carrie Underwood featured her adorable Min Pin, named Ace, in her wedding. Dressed in a pink tuxedo, Ace was photographed alongside a beaming Underwood at her wedding. In 2017, Ace suffered a herniated disc and was paralyzed for several days. Ace completed physical therapy, including water rehab, and is now living a happy life with his furry siblings, Penny and Zero.

Photo Courtesy
of Kyle Patrick Scanlon

Min Pins and Kids

Min Pins are small dogs with a dainty bone structure, which means they can be injured easily by adults and kids alike. Min Pins can be great with kids, as long as the children they interact with treat them with care, respect, and a gentle touch. But if they're handled roughly, especially during their formative months of socialization, they will have a negative and fearful reaction to most kids later in life. That's why it's so important to expose Min Pins to kids in those first few months, and to watch every interaction carefully so no one (your Min Pin or the kids) gets hurt. And that's why Min Pins tend to do better with older children, who are usually more attentive and careful with them.

You should always teach kids how to approach and touch your Min Pin. Teach them to approach your Min Pin slowly, from the side, and have them stop with enough room to allow the dog to come to the child. Having the child approach your Min Pin in a calm fashion with enough space will give the Min Pin the ability to watch the child without getting overwhelmed. Always, always supervise interactions between your Min Pin and young children— whether they're yours or someone else's.

When socializing your Min Pin with kids, it is imperative to be on alert for signs that your Min Pin might not be enjoying the interactions. Some red flags to teach them include growls, walking away from the child, resisting being held, retreating to a space where the child cannot get to the dog, etc. In addition, kids (and adults alike) should be on the lookout for body language from the dog. If you notice your Min Pin's tail is rigid, his ears are back, or the fur on his back is raised, then you should separate your Min Pin from the kids immediately.

No matter how friendly your Min Pin is, no dog should ever be left unsupervised with a child.

CHAPTER 7

Exercise for Your Miniature Pinscher

Types of Physical Exercise

You've just brought home a Min Pin, a very fitness-oriented, high-energy pup. Congratulations! You've inadvertently gotten yourself a workout buddy and your own fitness trainer. Just as there are a lot of ways for humans to exercise, there are also a lot of creative ways for your Miniature Pinscher to get the exercise he needs to work out all of his high energy. Daily

Photo Courtesy of Jacqueline Siotto-Zwirn

Photo Courtesy
of Katja Koho

walks, for starters, will be a must to meet your Min Pin's exercise needs and to show your Min Pin that you are the pack leader.

You can also entertain your Min Pin, get his heart rate going, and keep him calm by giving him short bursts of high intensity exercise (in human speak: high intensity impact training, but for dogs). When I first adopted Brady, he was extremely overweight, but not of his own doing. I could sense that there was an active, energetic dog inside him that was just dying to get out. He wasn't able to take long walks at first, since he was so overweight. At the time I adopted him, I was living in the Upper West Side of Manhattan, just off Broadway (a 4-lane road at that point in Manhattan). To get him the high intensity exercise he needed, every time we took a walk, we would sprint across Broadway on our way home. It was our favorite part of the walk. Eventually, those Broadway sprints became easy for him, so I would add short sprints into different parts of our walks to get him moving and to get his little heart pumping. He loved it, and so did I!

You can also play a lot of games with your Min Pin, like fetch or tug of war, and you can give your Min Pin different mental games for him to work with to keep his busy mind occupied.

Photo Courtesy of Evan Bolander

How Much Exercise Does Your Min Pin Need?

"During summer I fill a small pool with rubber balls, like the balls in a child's ball pit. Then I fill the pool part way with water. My Min Pins love it and it acclimates them to being in water. They cool themselves off and it conditions them to enjoying the water, making bath time easier."

JACQUELINE SIOTTO-ZWIRN
Sidels Miniature Pinschers

Because Min Pins are so lively and so smart, a typical adult Min Pin needs about 45-60 minutes per day of exercise. If they don't get enough exercise, Min Pins can engage in less than ideal behaviors, like digging, barking, destructive behaviors (like chewing or eliminating indoors), and escaping to play on their own.

When your Min Pin is just a puppy, he won't need quite as much exercise. A good general rule of thumb for puppies is that they need about 5 minutes of walking for every month of age, which would mean that a 4-month-old Min Pin would only need about 20 minutes of walking per day. Watch your Min Pin on the walk for signs of tiredness, like lagging behind, panting, or just lying down, and end the walk if it seems like he's had enough.

At least one or two daily walks are essential for your Min Pin to release any pent-up energy. These daily walks will allow your Min Pin to stimulate his mind, as he explores different sights, sounds, smells, and people/dogs he comes across. It will also create a strong bond between the two of you, where he realizes that you're his leader. If you establish this relationship with your Min Pin, he will be your loyal, lifetime follower. Depending on how much time you have in your day (and how old your Min Pin is), your walks can be 20 to 45 minutes, at a brisk pace. Dogs

CELEBRITY MIN PIN

Rusty the Surfing Min Pin

Rusty the surfing Min Pin is an Instagram celebrity with over thirteen thousand followers on the social networking site (@rustythesurfingminpin). But Rusty's fame goes beyond adorable pictures on the internet. This surfing dog won first place in the small dog category at the Petco Unleashed competition at Huntington Beach and took first place in Tandem with another dog named Giselle. Rusty was adopted from the Orange County Humane Society.

also love routine, so having a specific time or times carved out for your daily walks will keep your Min Pin happy and at ease.

One of the benefits of having a small dog (and there are many!) is that because Min Pins are so small, a lot of their exercise can happen indoors. You can chase each other around the house or the apartment, play fetch with his favorite toys, or spend time working on helping your Min Pin master new commands (see Chapter 8, Training Your Min Pin). This one-on-one playtime is just as important to your Min Pin's development as your walks outside together are, so make sure you set aside at least 10-20 minutes per day of dedicated playtime together.

Photo Courtesy of Annie Hughes

Another great way for your Min Pin to burn off some of his extra energy is to have him socialize with other puppies or friendly adult dogs. He will come home from a play session wiped out and ready to burrow under his blanket with you. Not only that, but it will help your Min Pin establish some great skills during his formative months that will last a lifetime.

Keeping Your Min Pin Mentally Engaged

Have you ever met a dog that is smarter than a lot of humans around him? If you haven't, that means you haven't spent much time with a Min Pin yet. You're in for a treat as you get to know your Min Pin. Not only will he be the most handsome, regal dog you've ever met, but he will outsmart any other dog (and sometimes you!).

My Min Pin, Brady, was as smart as can be. We had a lot of ways of communicating with each other. He would signal to me with his eyes when he wanted something. He had a whole system of whines to tell me what he was in the mood for. Even more astounding, though, was that he used to sneeze for "yes." Do you want to go for a walk? "Sneeze!" Go see Grandma and Grandpa? "Sneeze!" Take a bath? "Sneeze!" It was adorable. He always knew what was going on: if I had to go somewhere without him, if we were going together, or if he was staying somewhere else. He could just sense everything happening in our lives, and if he was excited about it, he would sneeze to let me know he was on board.

Because they're so smart, Min Pins need a lot of mental engagement and one-on-one playtime to keep their natural curiosity at bay. Here are some ideas for keeping your Min Pin mentally engaged:

- **Fetch**
  Playing fetch with your Min Pin allows him to burn some of his pent-up energy. Because they were originally bred for ratting, they love a good chase. You can play fetch with a small tennis ball, with his stuffed toys, or even with his bones. Playing fetch also instills a sense of loyalty in your Min Pin to his leader (you!). When he brings you the toy or the ball, he's showing you that he is your loyal friend bringing you his prey, and likewise, you're showing him that you can lead him. You can also find toys that will move about on their own—Min Pins respond well to this because they can use their natural prey drive by chasing the toy.

- **Tug of War**
  Min Pins love playing tug of war. It encourages their natural instinct to fight for their prey. Use a sturdy rope or soft toy, hold it in one hand and allow the Min Pin to pull on the other side. Give a little slack, take a

little slack, keeping him engaged the whole time. And allow him to take the object from you fully from time to time—that's the Min Pin's reward for doing his job. One other thing you may want to try as you train your Min Pin is to occasionally stop while you're playing and pet him, snuggle him, or just say "good boy." This will help him realize that, although he's fighting you for the object, you're still his best friend and supporter.

- **Puzzle Toys**

Puzzle toys are great for Min Pins because they challenge their minds and test their problem-solving skills. Most of them will involve food of some kind: you'll fill it with kibble, and your Min Pin has to figure out how to outsmart the toy to get to the food. There are also plush puzzle toys where one toy is hidden within another, and your Min Pin has to figure out how to get it out (a bit like Russian dolls, for dogs). Try out a few toys to see which kinds your Min Pin enjoys. He may need a bit of help solving them the first time, but once he knows the game, he will enjoy the hunt!

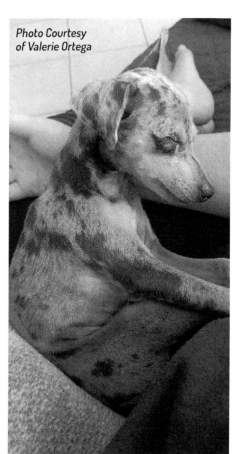

Photo Courtesy of Valerie Ortega

- **Kongs**

Kongs are a must-have for any dog owner. They're a great way to keep your Min Pin occupied. Fill your Kong with kibble, treats, or biscuits that tightly fit inside, along with peanut butter or plain yogurt, and you've given your Min Pin an activity to keep him engaged as well as treats to keep him happy. You can also try putting the Kong in the freezer, once you've filled it with yogurt and/or peanut butter. Then it becomes a cool treat that takes longer to work through.

- **Chew Toys**

Min Pins (and all dogs) love to chew because it releases endorphins, releases tension in the jaw, and helps them to relax. It also is a great way to keep them busy. Nylabone makes a lot of flavored, durable chew toys that your Min Pin will enjoy working on.

- ### *Scenting Games*
  Scenting and nose games will help your Min Pin hone his hunting game and provide good mental stimulation. You can start by hiding a few treats in a muffin tin, covering those treats with tennis balls, and then covering the remaining holes with tennis balls as well. Allow your Min Pin to start sniffing, uncover the treats, and enjoy the game. When he's finished, you can arrange the treats differently the next time and you've created a brand new game! You can also play the part of a magician, hiding treats under non-breakable cups, and allow your Min Pin to sniff out which ones are holding the treats.

- ### *Learning New Tricks*
  Teaching your Min Pin new commands and tricks is a great way to keep them mentally engaged. Sit, lie down, stay, fetch, up, high five...the list goes on! See Chapter 8 for more tips on training.

Bottom line: Min Pins are very smart little dogs, and your Min Pin needs an outlet for his mind. If Min Pins aren't provided with the mental stimulation they need, they'll find their own (usually destructive) ways to entertain themselves.

CHAPTER 8
Training Your Miniature Pinscher

Using Positive Reinforcement

In Chapter 5, we talked about the benefits of using positive reinforcement training for housetraining your Min Pin. But positive reinforcement training can go beyond your Min Pin's potty usage: you can use it for all of his training needs.

So what is positive reinforcement training? A pet will learn something when he's able to understand the relationship between his behavior and the consequences that follow. If there is a positive relationship between his behavior and the consequences (e.g., treats, praise, or other reward), your Min Pin will likely continue performing the behavior in order to get the desired reward. My Min Pin, Brady, was very food motivated, so for him, treats were a great positive reinforcement tool. For other dogs, a pat on the head, a play session, a walk, a toy, or a treat may be the right motivation.

The trick with positive reinforcement is that the reward you're giving your Min Pin must happen *immediately* after he's accomplished the desired behavior. For example, if you teach your Min Pin to "sit" and you give him that command, you must give him the treat before he stands up—otherwise, he might think that standing up is the desired behavior.

Make sure the rewards you offer are varied and are things that appeal to your Min Pin. When you're working on a new command or bigger behavioral issues (like potty training), offer yummy treats that are set aside for these special occasions. As your Min Pin gets better at the desired behavior, you can transition him to his regular treats, or offer playtime with his favorite toy as a reward. And always, always offer lots of praise.

Consistency and patience are two qualities you'll need as you use positive reinforcement training. Sure, it can be

FUN FACT
What's In A Name?

Miniature Pinschers originated in Germany, where they were called "Zwergpinscher" or "little biter." When Min Pins were introduced in America, they were simply referred to as "Pinscher" (meaning "Toy") until 1972 when they officially became the "Miniature Pinscher."

*Photo Courtesy
of Misenna Messinger*

frustrating to have your Min Pin disobey your commands. But showing your anger and disappointment with your Min Pin will not help—punishment and fear only distance your dog from you and confuse him as to what the appropriate behavior is. When you get frustrated, take a deep breath, take a moment away from your Min Pin, and start training again when you're feeling more calm and relaxed. Your Min Pin will be happier to work with a relaxed, positive parent.

Positive reinforcement training will help you to build trust with your Min Pin over time. By rewarding positive behavior, you can help your Min Pin find a sense of pride in exhibiting good behavior, and it will create a bond between your Min Pin and you so you feel like a team. When you create that association between your Min Pin doing the right thing and you showering him with affection, treats, or other rewards, your Min Pin will look to find other ways to work with you and win your admiration.

Basic Commands

Whether you've got a Min Pin puppy or you adopted an older Min Pin, teaching your Min Pin basic commands is a must. When I adopted my Min Pin, Brady, he was over seven years old and still didn't know basic commands. Every night, when I came home from work, I would feed him his dinner, take him for a walk, and spend 10 minutes training him after we got home. Over a period of just a few weeks, he knew "sit" and "stay" and "lie down." And with even more time, he knew a lot more. See? You can teach an old dog new tricks. All it took was consistency, patience, and positivity.

Here are some basic commands you can work on with your Min Pin:

Sit

You can teach your Min Pin to sit using one of two methods. You can stand in front of him and say "sit" until he does, at which point you give him a treat. Or, you kneel or sit at eye level with him, holding a treat in front of him, and slowly move the treat above his head so he has to sit his bottom down and lift his head to get to the treat. When his bottom touches the ground, you can give him the treat. Repeat this a few times, and start saying "sit" before his bottom touches the ground. Never push your Min Pin's bottom to the ground—forcing him into position may just confuse him, and since he's just a little guy, he could be injured with a small amount of force.

Down

You can teach your Min Pin "Down" very similarly to "sit." You can stand over your Min Pin, give the command for him to lie down, wait for him to lie down, and reinforce the behavior with a treat when he does. You can also lure him to the ground by holding the treat in your hand, close to your Min Pin's nose, and slowly bring it to the floor. When he is down on his belly, you can give him the treat. When he can reliably follow your hand signal, begin saying "down" as you move your hand.

Stay

A dog that knows "stay" will remain sitting until you ask him to get up by giving another cue, called the "release word." The goal is to teach your Min Pin to remain sitting until the release cue is given, and then begin adding distance. First, teach your Min Pin the release word that you choose, like "okay" or "free." Stand with your puppy as he sits, toss a treat on the floor near your feet, and say your release word as he steps forward to get the treat. Repeat this until you're able to say the word first and then toss the treat after he moves. When your Min Pin knows the release cue, have him sit, face him, say "stay," and give him a treat. Say "stay" again, pause, and give him another treat for staying seated. Then release him with your release command. Over time, start to increase the time you wait between treats, and then start to add distance between the two of you. The more solidly your Min Pin learns to stay, the longer he can remain sitting, even while you're off doing other tasks.

Come

To train your Min Pin to "come," you'll want to be indoors. Sit a few feet away from your Min Pin and say his name and then "come." When he comes to you, give him a treat and praise. It's that easy! Gradually increase the distance between you and your Min Pin when you ask him to "come," until you can eventually call him from room to room. You can also ask a friend or a partner to help by gently holding your Min Pin's collar while you walk away a longer distance and then call your Min Pin to you (giving him treats and praise when he does). Once your Min Pin is consistently coming to you inside the house, you can practice "come" outdoors, on a long leash if you do not have a fenced-in yard.

Leave it

"Leave it" is an especially helpful cue for dogs that are easily distracted or disturbed. For a Min Pin, who was bred to hunt rats and other small animals, bunnies and squirrels can cause quite a distraction while you're out walking. "Leave it" can

Photo Courtesy
of Ilona Kolossova

also help your Min Pin ignore random food you might see on your walks. (I can't tell you how many times, living in Manhattan, I had to cue Brady to leave chicken bones and other garbage we'd see on the sidewalk.) To teach "leave it," place a row of treats your Min Pin isn't overly excited about on the ground, several feet apart, with your Min Pin out of the room. Put your Min Pin on a leash and bring him into the room, saying "leave it" as you walk him past the row of treats. For every treat he ignores, give him a high value treat and praise, then walk along to the next treat. If your Min Pin tries to go for the floor treat, cover it with your foot and gently guide him away from it with the leash. You can repeat this exercise outside in your yard, and try swapping the treats for a bone, a toy, or a ball. The more things he is taught to "leave" in and around your house, the better he'll do with real-world situations.

There are many more cues you can give your Min Pin to work on, but the key is not to expect success all at once and not to overload your Min Pin with too many tasks at the outset. Training works best in increments, when you focus on one task at a time. Make sure you keep your training sessions brief (no more than 10 minutes) and end a session early if your Min Pin seems bored or frustrated. Always end on a positive note—if he knows one cue well, make sure he gets a treat and praise for doing it at the end of your session.

Dealing with Unwanted Behaviors

Your Min Pin, while handsome, intelligent, and generally fun to be around, may exhibit some unwanted behaviors, whether it's a behavior he already exhibited when you got him or something he's taken to since he moved into your home. When this happens, the important thing to remember is that he's looking for attention—he just doesn't have words to express it.

Take my Min Pin, Brady, as an example. We had a fairly consistent routine for a couple of years. I worked 10-hour days, 5 days per week. He had a dog walker and doggy day care while I was at work. But when I was at home, he was my number one priority. Eventually, we moved, and I took a different job that required fewer hours during the day, but I had started to work on the side as a yoga teacher and a wellness coach. My evenings were full of yoga classes and client appointments, instead of full-time Brady care. I still made sure he got the same number and duration of walks, the same feeding schedule, etc. But what was missing for him was quality time together. He sent me the message one night after I had walked him and went off to meet a client. He had already done his business on our walk (numbers one and two), but when I came home, right in the middle of the living room was

Photo Courtesy of Maria Björn

a log of dog poo. He wasn't ill, and he certainly knew how to hold his bowels. It was a message to me: Mom, you're not giving me enough attention. I listened, and I started spacing out my appointments better to make more time for Brady and me.

When you're dealing with unwanted behavior from your Min Pin, first try to investigate and understand why your Min Pin is acting in the way that he's acting. Once you know why, then you can come up with a solution. Try to figure out what motivates your Min Pin—is it treats? Praise? Quality time? More walks?

Keep in mind that sometimes, you may inadvertently be encouraging an unwanted behavior like barking, jumping, or scratching simply by giving attention to your Min Pin while he's doing it. Giving your Min Pin food, physical affection, or playing with him in an attempt to calm him down while he's engaged in unwanted behavior will only reinforce the problem behavior.

Try to be patient and consistent. The more significant the unwanted behavior, the longer it can be before you and your Min Pin work through a solution. And be consistent with your Min Pin's training and behaviors. Everyone in your household must be on the same page in training, expectations, and reactions.

Always be kind to your Min Pin. No matter what the behavior, never hit, scream at, or get physical with your dog. Reacting in anger and creating fear in your Min Pin will never solve the problem.

When to Hire a Trainer

When it feels like you need help with training your Min Pin, or you've got some unwanted problem behaviors you haven't been able to resolve on your own, a great dog trainer can make all the difference. This isn't a failure on your part as a dog owner; it just means your Min Pin needs a little more than you're able to give him right now. A trainer can aid in helping your Min Pin master basic commands, or if your Min Pin engages in behaviors like soiling inside the house, running away from the house when you open the door, jumping on people as they enter, pulling on the leash, or guarding his objects.

A good trainer can help your Min Pin's behavior and create a stronger bond between you and your Min Pin by helping you troubleshoot your problems and hone your abilities as a dog owner.

How do you find a good trainer? First, you should know that dog training is completely unregulated, which means anyone can charge for their services as a dog trainer, regardless of their education or experience. That's why it's important to do your research and speak with any potential trainers before you sign on to work with them. Here's a list of things to consider before you hire a trainer:

- *References and Recommendations*
  If you've bought your Min Pin from a breeder, he or she will have a list of trainers that you could work with. Your veterinarian's office will also have a list of people they can recommend. A good trainer will have plenty of people who can act as references for him or her.

- *Training Philosophy*
  Ask the trainer about his or her methods and training philosophy, and make sure you look for a trainer who uses positive reinforcement training.

- *Specified Services*
  Make sure you know what it is that you are looking for from your trainer (Basic commands? Leash training? Jumping?). Not all trainers will offer the same services, and you'll need to find one that works specifically with your Min Pin's needs.

- *Education And Credentials*
  Ask the potential trainer about his or her education and credentials. While certification with the Certification Council of Professional Dog Trainers isn't mandatory, it would show the trainer's dedication and interest in continuing education.

- *Personality*
  Make sure you find a trainer that you'll want to work with personality-wise. Dog training isn't just for your Min Pin; the trainer will work with

you to teach you how to work with your Min Pin. As such, you'll want to make sure you feel comfortable learning from this person.

If your Min Pin exhibits signs of aggression (growling, snapping, biting, etc.) or anxiety, you should set up an appointment with your veterinarian. He or she may recommend more than just training, like working with a veterinary behaviorist and/or giving your Min Pin medication to help ease his temperament.

Photo Courtesy
of Cheyenne Byers
Coastal Paradise Pinschers

CHAPTER 9
Nutrition for Your Miniature Pinscher

The Importance of a Good Diet

Having a good diet for your Min Pin is essential for his health. Just like us humans, Min Pins (and all dogs) need a proper balance of protein, carbohydrates, fats, vitamins, minerals, and water each day.

A good diet keeps your Min Pin fit and healthy. Proteins, for example, help your Min Pin with muscle function and growth, while also repairing damaged cells and making new ones. Fats provide energy, help the brain perform its functions, and keep your Min Pin's coat shiny and healthy. Carbohydrates give your Min Pin a quick source of energy to burn for his high activity level, as well as provide fiber to help with digestion and elimination. Vitamins and minerals work to keep your Min Pin's immune system healthy and his metabolism functioning normally, preventing disease and helping with muscle contraction and nerve condition.

All of these essential nutrients, plus an adequate amount of water, are necessary to provide your Min Pin with optimal health, now and in the future.

Talking with Your Veterinarian about Diet

Talking to your veterinarian about your Min Pin's diet should be the first step in making sure your Min Pin has a good diet, and a good veterinarian will ask you at every well visit about what you're feeding your Min Pin, how much, and how often.

Your vet can help you choose a quality commercial food, help you understand the basic requirements of a home diet, give you a rough estimate of how many calories your Min Pin might need, etc., so that you make sure you meet your Min Pin's nutritional needs during his various life stages. Your vet will take into account age, body condition, and activity level in making recommendations, plus the vet may have a preference on foods based on his or her own experience in working with other dogs' diets.

Your vet can also advise you on how many treats you should give your dog, what kind of ingredients to steer clear of, etc. And your vet should give you a list of foods never to feed your dog, like chocolate, raisins, and a few others (see Treats and People Food, below).

Choosing a Quality Commercial Food

A good diet is one of the best ways to keep your Min Pin healthy and make sure his most basic needs are met nutritionally. Pet food manufacturers work hard to determine the exact formula that goes into their products so that they provide everything your dog needs on a daily basis. Choosing the right commercial food can be tough, however, because there are thousands of dog food options available. And opinions can vary between breeders, vets, trainers, and just about every article you find on the internet. So how do you choose a quality commercial food for your Min Pin?

You'll need to consider factors like type of food, quality of ingredients, and cost to make sure the food fits within your budget. Feeding a dog (even a small one like a Min Pin) can be almost as expensive as feeding a human if you get too carried away with all of the bells and whistles.

The "best" food for your Min Pin doesn't have to be the fanciest or most expensive. Here are some tips for picking the right food for your Min Pin:

- *Choosing wet or dry food.* For purposes of nutrition and digestibility, there isn't a difference between wet and dry dog food. You should make your decision based on your lifestyle, preferences, and budget. For dogs that need more water, have problems chewing, or have certain special dietary needs, canned foods may be a better choice. Otherwise, most Min Pins will do fine on dry kibble.

- *Read the ingredient label.* Dog food ingredient labels are less user-friendly than human ingredient labels, and deciphering them may be challenging, but make

Photo Courtesy of Robert Bienvenu

sure you read them anyway. Pet food ingredients are listed by order of weight, so that means that if an ingredient is listed first, there is more of that ingredient than the ones that follow. Make sure you select a diet for your Min Pin that has real, recognizable, whole-food ingredients. If the majority of listed ingredients is unfamiliar to you, find another type of food.

- *Look for a food that is formulated to your Min Pin's life stage—puppy, young adult, adult, senior, etc.* Those foods will have different nutritional content intended to target your dog's stage of life. A puppy will need more energy, so he'll require more calories and nutrients to support growing muscles, whereas a senior dog will need much less to sustain him but may require different nutrients to keep him healthy.

- *Consider a food formulated for your Min Pin's small size.* Larger dogs and small dogs are not built alike, and small dogs like Min Pins may do better with small, bite-sized kibble.

- *Find the right food for your Min Pin's activity level.* If your Min Pin is like most Min Pins, he is a very active little boy. The King of Toys loves to run, play, jump, and stay active for a large part of the day. Finding a food that will support his activity level and his athleticism is key. But if your Min Pin is a bit older, or doesn't get as much exercise, you may want to consider a lower calorie food that offers weight management while still keeping your dog well fed.

- *Address your Min Pin's special needs, if any.* As you get to know your Min Pin, you'll start to notice whether he has any special needs. Does he have problems with digestion? Does he have seasonal allergies? Does he have sensitive skin? Does your Min Pin have any special health conditions? There are foods made to target a lot of these conditions nutritionally.

Once you've done your research, and talked to your veterinarian, the last step to determine whether you've found the "right" food for your Min Pin is to make sure he enjoys it. Watch him while he eats, and see if he eats with enthusiasm or walks away from the food after you've set it down. Also, keep an eye on his activity level versus his energy on his diet. If he's not getting enough nutrients, he might be lethargic. If he is getting too many, you might notice a bit of weight gain.

Just like we, as humans, need to watch what we eat and make sure to feed ourselves without overdoing it, we have to do the same for our Min Pins to keep them safe and healthy.

Preparing Your Own Dog Food

If you have the time, the energy, and the money to cook for yourself and your Min Pin, then making homemade dog food should be a fun experiment! But make sure you do your research on your Min Pin's nutritional needs and talk to your veterinarian ahead of time.

Your Min Pin needs protein (animal meat, seafood, dairy, or eggs), fat (from meat or oil), and carbohydrates (from grains or vegetables). He'll also need calcium (from dairy or eggshells) and essential fatty acids (from plant oils, egg yolks, oatmeal, and other foods). And your Min Pin will need supplements if you're only feeding him from scratch—which ones you give him will depend on which nutrients are missing from his meals.

There are plenty of dog food recipes and feeding plans on the internet, but the best way to make sure a recipe and a food plan has the nutritional content your Min Pin needs is to choose one created by an expert with training in dog nutrition, like a certified pet nutritionist. And you can also set up an appointment to talk with a nutritionist to make sure you're getting it right. Also make sure to consult with your vet first.

Once your Min Pin has been on a homemade diet for a couple of weeks, take him to the vet to make sure your dog isn't gaining or losing weight. You may need to adjust quantities to account for weight loss or gain. If so, take him for a weight check again in a couple of weeks to make sure you're on the right track.

The best way to ensure you're feeding your Min Pin well is to take him for his wellness visits twice a year if on a homemade diet. The vet can look at skin, coat, and body condition, and may also want to run bloodwork to make sure the diet you're feeding your pup isn't having any adverse effects on him internally.

Raw Food and Grain-Free Diets

Raw food and grain-free diets have become increasingly popular among dog owners. A raw dog food diet generally consists of raw meats (both organ and muscle meats), whole or ground bones, raw eggs, fruits and vegetables, and some dairy. People who tout a raw food diet for their dogs claim that they have shinier coats, healthier skin, increased energy, better dental health, and better digestion. If you decide to try a raw food diet, make sure you clear it with your veterinarian first.

Feeding your Min Pin a raw food diet requires you to handle, prepare, and sanitize raw food in a very mindful way so your pup doesn't get sick.

Photo Courtesy of Karis Antokal

It can be both time consuming and expensive.

For safety reasons, it is not recommended in homes with small children or immunocompromised people, since they could get sick from the health risks of raw foods like salmonella, E-coli, and other bacteria contamination. The American Veterinary Medical Association has taken a formal position against unregulated feeding of raw food to dogs because of the risk of illness.

A grain-free diet, on the other hand, might not pose as many obvious health risks for your Min Pin, but you should still talk with your vet about it first. A grain-free diet will replace traditional grains (like corn, soy, rice, barley, and other grains) with other foods (like peas, lentils, potatoes, and sweet potatoes). A grain-free diet might be helpful, for example, for a dog that has allergies, to help reduce the amount of foods in his diet that might trigger allergic reactions. Or, you might want to select a grain-free food for your Min Pin because it seems to have higher quality ingredients.

Taking grains out of your Min Pin's diet, however, might be riskier than you'd think. The Food and Drug Administration released a warning in 2019 that grain-free foods could be related to a life-threatening heart problem in dogs called dilated cardiomyopathy (DCM). The study was based on 515 dogs who developed DCM, and 90% of these dogs had been on grain-free diets. While there is no proof that the grain-free diets caused the incidences of DCM, the FDA still issued a caution that it's investigating the link between the two.

Bottom line: if you choose to feed your Min Pin a raw food or a grain-free diet, consult your veterinarian first.

Treats and People Food

We all love giving our dog treats, both for training purposes and because, well, it's our way of showing affection. How do you choose the proper treats for your Min Pin? Choose treats that are specially formulated for dogs, since they're designed to be tasty without upsetting your Min Pin's tummy. You can

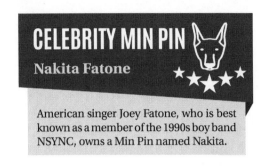

CELEBRITY MIN PIN

Nakita Fatone

American singer Joey Fatone, who is best known as a member of the 1990s boy band NSYNC, owns a Min Pin named Nakita.

also look for treats that have added nutrients or dental benefits.

A good rule of thumb is to try to keep treats to only about 10% of your Min Pin's diet. That means that 90% of his main nutrition should come from his food, and a mere 10% should come from treats. Since your Min Pin is so small, you may want to look for smaller treats. Generally, the bigger the treat, the more calories it has, so those giant bone treats are going to be a lot for your tiny guy, no matter how much he likes them.

You can also give your dog treats in the form of veggies, like carrots, green beans, broccoli, or the like. They're low in calories and high in fiber. My Min Pin, Brady, loved veggies of all kinds. Carrots were his favorite, but he got almost just as excited for kale stems and Brussels sprout leaves.

You can also give your Min Pin other human foods like peanut butter (as long as it's not sweetened with xylitol) and plain yogurt as treats—they work great in Kongs as a distraction tool. And the occasional piece of meat or fish that you're having at dinner can be a wonderful treat to show how much you love them. (Make sure you never feed your Min Pin while you're eating, and he'll learn not to expect food from you during that time.)

But proceed with caution: some foods that are harmless to humans can be harmful or toxic to dogs. Never feed your Min Pin onions, garlic, chocolate, grapes, raisins, avocados, macadamia nuts, or stone fruit pits. Read all labels on items like candy, gum, toothpaste, and peanut butter to make sure you're not accidentally feeding your dog xylitol (a sweetener that is toxic to dogs and can cause liver failure). Try to avoid sugary treats of all kinds. And while bones from the meat you cook for yourself seem like a wonderful treat for your Min Pin, they are actually a high risk food that can splinter and block or tear your Min Pin's digestive system.

Ask your vet about other people foods before offering them to your Min Pin—they should have a list of foods to never feed your dog. Keep that list on your refrigerator as a handy reference of foods to avoid giving your precious best friend!

Weight Management

"Do not over feed; Pins are the Piranhas of the dog world. They will eat everything until they are engorged, so watch what you feed them and do it on a schedule. DO NOT free feed! You will have an obese dog that won't live very long."

JACQUELINE SIOTTO-ZWIRN
Sidels Miniature Pinschers

Plenty of dog owners think that food equals love, and that giving your dog more treats just shows him how much you love him. It's understandable to feel that way and to want to treat your special, handsome Min Pin with all the love he can handle. However (and this is a big however), food can't always be the way. Take it from me. My Min Pin, Brady, came to me as an obese dog. He weighed 18 pounds! How did he get that way? All I really know about his prior life was that he lived with an older woman until she passed away. I'm guessing that she didn't get him much exercise, and she didn't control his food intake. After I adopted Brady, with a good diet and plenty of exercise, I was able to help him get down to 12 pounds over time.

Photo Courtesy
of Ilona Kolossova

It's hard to say what effects his obesity had on his health in the long run, but it was easy to see how much happier and more lively he was when he was down to a healthy weight.

To keep something like this from happening with your own Min Pin, ask your veterinarian to evaluate your Min Pin's size at each checkup. Once your Min Pin reaches maturity, he should weigh between 8 and 10 pounds, according to the American Kennel Club. As a rule of thumb, if your Min Pin is between 0% and 15% above that weight (more than 10 but less than 11.5 pounds), he'll be considered overweight. More than 15% above that weight (more than 11.5 pounds) and he'll be considered obese.

In between vet visits, you should weigh your Min Pin periodically to make sure he's keeping a good weight. Most vets are happy to let you use the scale at the office anytime, or you can use a scale at home. You can hold your Min Pin while you weigh yourself (and subtract your own weight from the total), or you could invest in a baby scale. Regardless of which method you use, make sure you use the same scale consistently to keep track of your Min Pin's weight.

If you find that your Min Pin is overweight, you'll need to evaluate your Min Pin's diet. Are you feeding him too much dog food? Too many treats? Too much people food? Knowing the right amount of food to give your dog is imperative for keeping him healthy. Always ask your vet for advice on how often and how much to feed your Min Pin.

Also key to weight management is making sure your Min Pin has enough daily exercise. He needs to walk, run, and play every day, even on the days when you're not feeling much like doing any of those things (see Chapter 7, Exercise for your Miniature Pinscher, for recommendations on how much and what kind of exercise he needs). If your Min Pin is gaining weight, try adding in an extra 10 minutes of walking or jogging each day to his normal exercise routine. It will be good for both of you!

If cutting out unhealthy snacks and increasing physical activity don't help your Min Pin lose weight, it's possible that an underlying health condition may have triggered the weight gain. That's why it's important to check with your vet. They'll run blood tests that will look for a low thyroid level and hormonal imbalances, among other things.

Keeping your Min Pin at a good weight is important, not just because you want him to remain the svelte, handsome King of Toys that you brought home, but also because obesity can contribute to a whole list of health problems in dogs, such as trouble breathing, heat stroke, pancreatitis, diabetes, orthopedic concerns, reduction in lifespan, skin conditions, heart problems, and the like. Trust me: you'll want to keep your Min Pin with you as long as possible, and having him live a healthy life is worth cutting back on a few treats.

CHAPTER 10
Grooming Your Miniature Pinscher

Coat Care Basics

Min Pins have a short, hard coat that is very easy to maintain. Min Pins generally don't need regular haircuts, shaves, or trims. Instead, your Min Pin will need regular brushing to keep shedding to a minimum and keep his coat shiny. With a new puppy (or even an adult Min Pin), the time you spend together grooming him will help strengthen the bond between you and help accustom him to being touched and worked with. Frequent bathing isn't recommended because it dries the skin, but it's okay to bathe your Min Pin when he rolls in something smelly or is very dirty.

Note that the only time you should attempt to shave or shorten your Min Pin's coat is with the guidance and supervision of your veterinarian. This might need to happen, for example, for medical issues, such as your vet trying to get a better look at skin issues or shaving to put an IV in for surgery. Otherwise, there's no reason to trim your Min Pin's hair!

Photo Courtesy
of Kimberley Diver and Dale Hacking

Bathing Your Min Pin

"Min Pins only need bathing if their coats get noticeably dirty. They don't need weekly baths like longer haired dogs. Bathing them to frequently will dry out their skin."

KAREN MERICA
Lilbears Kennels

In addition to having a short coat that is easy to maintain with very little grooming, Min Pins generally don't need to be bathed very often. If your Min Pin somehow gets dirty on a walk or rolls in something unpleasant, you will need to bathe him straight away. But otherwise, bathing your Min Pin once a month should be enough to keep him clean, shiny, and feeling great.

When you're bathing your Min Pin, make sure you have a good pre-bath routine established. First, you'll want to tire him out before his bath because that King of Toys might be too wired for a bath if you don't expend some of his energy beforehand. Second, brush your Min Pin before bath time to keep hair in your bathtub to a minimum.

When you do get him into the bathtub, keep in mind that he'll need a warm (but not too hot) temperature to make sure he doesn't get too cold. A couple of inches of water at the bottom of the tub should be enough for your Min Pin. Using a cup, pour some water over your pup's head and body, wetting him down. Next, shampoo your Min Pin: work the shampoo in a lather, and massage the shampoo into his skin, in the same way you'd wash and massage your own hair. Let the shampoo sit on your dog's coat for several minutes before thoroughly rinsing with fresh water from the faucet. Make sure you avoid the eyes and the face, and make sure only to use shampoo that is specifically formulated for dogs (people shampoo and conditioner are not safe for pets).

And watch his ears—because of their upright ears, it's easy for soap to

Photo Courtesy
of Hege Isabella

84

get into a Min Pin's ear canal. Make sure you rinse the ears thoroughly and make sure there's no leftover soap in their ears after bath time.

When you're finished, towel-dry your Min Pin for as long as he'll tolerate it. One of my favorite times with Brady was after his bath. I'd wrap him up like a baby in a towel and carry him around like a newborn for as long as he'd let me. When he'd had enough, I'd set him down and let him zoom around the apartment. He would rub his face and body all over every rug and blanket he could find, and then he'd pant with excitement and run some more. Eventually, when he got his post-bath energy out, he'd cuddle in with me to stay warm.

Photo Courtesy
of Jacqueline Siotto-Zwirn

Brushing Your Min Pin

Min Pins have a short, hard, and wiry coat. Compared to longer-haired dogs, there is not a lot of heavy shedding, but Min Pins still do shed from their coats. Brush your Min Pin about twice a week with a soft brush or a grooming mitt to help remove any dead hair. It will also help to keep your home, furniture, and clothing (relatively) free of dog hair. Regular brushing also helps to distribute your Min Pin's natural skin oils, which will leave his coat shiny and healthy.

Trimming Nails

"Trim their nails at least every two weeks. Get them used to this as early as possible. If you get your puppy at 8 weeks old, start trimming their nails that week and do it regularly so they learn to deal with it early on."

JACQUELINE SIOTTO-ZWIRN
Sidels Miniature Pinschers

Min Pins can grow longer nails than some other breeds, which means you'll need to trim them regularly to keep them comfortable for your Min Pin. If his nails become too long, it can grow painful for him to walk. Aim to trim your Min Pin's nails every few weeks.

That said, Brady never had to have his nails trimmed. When we went to the vet, they always remarked on how well-groomed his nails were. The two of us walked a lot, mostly on pavement, and those long walks wore down his nails. So if you and your Min Pin also walk a fair amount on sidewalks and paved roads, listen to whether you can hear your Min Pin's nails when he walks across the floor. If yes, you'll need to trim them. If not, no trim necessary.

If you've never clipped a dog's nails before, you should ask your vet to show you how to do it properly. To clip your Min Pin's nails, you'll first need to get a nail clipper designed for a small dog breed; these tend to be the best for controlling how short you end up cutting the nails. Make sure you (and a partner, if available) are able to hold your Min Pin firmly and keep a good grip on the paw you'd like to trim. Next, push back any fur that is in the way of the nail and carefully place the opening of the nail clippers over the end of the nail. To avoid getting the "quick"—where the blood vessels run through the nail—try trimming a little of the nail off at a time. Min Pins have black claws, which makes it harder to eye the quick, so start with a little bit on each nail. If you are able to cut that amount safely off one nail, you can probably cut the same amount safely with another nail. Keep an eye out for nails that are more worn down than others, as they will require less clipping than the longer ones.

If this seems too intimidating, you can trust your vet to trim your Min Pin's nails, or you can take him regularly to see a professional groomer.

Photo Courtesy of Nicole Gray

Cleaning Eyes, Ears, and Teeth

You should also attend to your Min Pin's eyes, ears, and teeth regularly to keep him well-groomed. On a daily basis, you can check his eyes for debris (usually coming from the inside corner of his eyes). If there is debris or runniness, you can use a warm damp cotton ball or a soft washcloth to wipe around the eyes and remove any dirt or other goopy substances that have built up.

Your Min Pin's ears should be checked at least weekly for redness or a bad odor, which can be a signal of infection. When you check your Min Pin's ears, wipe them with a cotton ball that's been moistened with a gentle, pH-balanced dog-specific ear cleaner to help prevent infections (ask your vet for recommendations). Just clean the outer ear (any part of the ear that you can see). Never insert anything into your Min Pin's ear canal.

As for your Min Pin's teeth, brush them at least a few times a week (if not daily) to remove tartar buildup and bacteria, and to prevent gum disease and bad breath.

Start by getting your Min Pin used to brushing when you first bring him home. Give him a little dog-approved toothpaste on your finger and make sure he likes the taste of it. (Note: Never use human toothpaste, as it can contain xylitol, a sweetener that is toxic for dogs). Next time you get out the toothpaste, you can put your finger in his mouth and begin to gently rub his teeth and gums with toothpaste. From there, you can move onto a finger brush, and once he's accepted all these methods of brushing, you can start brushing his teeth with a dog toothbrush. You can also use positive reinforcement when you're finished (like a game of tug of war or a bone) as a reward for allowing you to groom him in this special way. Over time, your Min Pin might love having his teeth brushed!

> ## FUN FACT
> **Min Pin Mascot**
>
> In 2017, a small company called Beer Paws adopted a Min Pin named Luseal as its unofficial mascot. Luseal, who was rescued from a shelter in Texas by Heartstrings Animal Advocates, was originally only supposed to stay with her foster mom for about 10 days, but at the end of that time, the founder of Beer Paws, Crystal Wiebe, just couldn't say goodbye. Luseal joined Crystal's two other dogs in her new forever home instead!

CHAPTER 11

Healthcare for Miniature Pinschers

Regular Vet Visits and Prevention

All dogs—including Min Pins—should have a complete physical exam at least once a year. Taking your Min Pin to his annual veterinary exams will allow you to make informed choices about his health and well-being, and you'll also be able to find out about illnesses or other health issues early.

Photo Courtesy of Kyle Patrick Scanlon

During your Min Pin's annual wellness exams, the vet will listen to your Min Pin's heart and lungs, examine his eyes, ears, and teeth, and check for fleas or other common issues. The vet will also keep your Min Pin up-to-date on his vaccinations and make recommendations for activities and medications specific to your Min Pin's needs.

Common Diseases and Conditions

All dogs have the potential to develop genetic health problems (just like all people have the potential to inherit a particular disease). The Min Pin is prone to some health problems, including:

- *Progressive Retinal Atrophy (PRA)*
  PRA is an eye disease that involves the gradual deterioration of the retina (a thin layer of tissue that lines the back of the eye on the inside). Dogs with PRA are night-blind and may lose sight during the day when they reach advanced stages of the condition. There is currently no effective treatment available for PRA.

- *Legg-Calve-Perthes Disease*
  Legg-Calve-Perthes Disease is caused by the decrease of blood supply to the femur (the thigh bone). As the disease progresses, the head of the femur (the ball part of the hip's ball and socket joint) disintegrates. The first sign of Legg-Calve-Perthes, limping, usually appears when the puppy is 4 to 6 months old. In many cases, treatment requires surgery to remove the head of the leg bone.

- *Patellar Luxation*
  Patellar luxation is a common issue in small dogs, and it refers to when the kneecap (patella) shifts out of its joint because the groove is too narrow. If that happens, the dog may cry out in pain when running or walking. The symptoms may come and go, but may require surgery. An OFA evaluation can rule out patellar luxation.

- *MPS VI*
  The most serious condition that affects the Miniature Pinscher is a rare disorder known as mucopolysaccharidosis, or MPS VI. It's a genetic defect affecting the way the body processes certain sugar molecules, and a build-up of unprocessed sugar molecules can result in joint deformity, eye cloudiness, and facial deformity. Breeding two carriers can produce affected puppies, so make sure you receive documentation from a breeder who can give you written documentation from the Josephine Deubler Genetic Disease Testing Laboratory at the University of Pennsylvania that the Min Pin's parents were not carriers. Bone mar-

Photo Courtesy
of Sharron Cook

row treatment at a young age can be an effective (but expensive) treatment, and enzyme replacement therapy might also be effective, but is not yet widely used in animals.

- *Hypothyroidism*
Min Pins can experience hypothyroidism, or an underactive thyroid. Symptoms may include obesity, hair loss, seizures and/or lethargy. Hypothyroidism can be diagnosed by your vet with a simple blood test and regulated with medication.

- *Allergies*
Min Pins are prone to skin allergies, which can lead to itchy skin and bacterial skin infections. The best way to treat an allergy is to avoid the cause and allergen, and will depend on your pup's type of allergy. For example, the best way to treat a food allergy or food intolerance is a change in diet. Your vet might also suggest an allergy relief medication for your Min Pin.

Not all of these conditions are detectable in a growing puppy, and it can be hard to predict whether an animal will be free of these maladies. This is why, if you get your Min Pin from a breeder, you must find a reputable breeder who is committed to breeding the healthiest Min Pins (see Chapter 1). Careful breeders will screen their breeding dogs for genetic disease, and use only the healthiest and best-looking dogs for breeding. However, even the healthiest of parents and a guarantee from a breeder is no guarantee from Mother Nature—your Min Pin might develop one of these diseases, despite all breeding efforts. But the good news is that advances in veterinary medicine mean that, in most cases, even if your Min Pin develops any issues, he can still live a good life.

My Min Pin, Brady, was the opposite of a healthy specimen when I adopted him. He was morbidly obese. He had bad allergies and constant skin infections (so much so that his hair fell out and you could see bald, red, flaky patches on his skin). He had periodontal disease that literally made his teeth rot from the inside out. He was a mess when I adopted him, and, quite honestly, I wasn't sure if he'd make it another year when I got him. But over time, with a special diet, a lot of exercise, some dental surgery, frequent baths, and quite a few trips to the vet, Brady turned into a healthy, happy, fit, and loving little guy. We were able to spend many years adventuring together, happily and healthily so.

Photo Courtesy of Nicole Grey

Monitoring

Aside from taking your Min Pin to his annual wellness exams, you are the best tool around for making sure your Min Pin stays healthy. Here's a list of things you can keep track of as a Min Pin parent:

- *Regular weight checks.* Weigh your Min Pin regularly to make sure he's not gaining or losing too much weight.
- *Appetite.* Check on your Min Pin's appetite and level of interest in food. Is your Min Pin hungrier than normal? Is he turning food away?
- *Vomiting or diarrhea.* One of the most unpleasant (and not uncommon) things to deal with is stomach issues with your pup. Keep an eye out for vomiting and diarrhea.
- *Skin and itching.* Watch out for changes in your Min Pin's skin condition, like redness, flaking, or excessive itching.
- *Energy level.* Keep a regular eye on your Min Pin's energy level. Does your Min Pin seem more or less energetic than normal?
- *Sleep.* Notice how long and how often your Min Pin sleeps. Is your Min Pin sleeping more hours per day than usual?
- *Behavior.* Keep an eye out for unusual behaviors. Is your Min Pin more aggressive than normal? Or is he hiding under furniture?
- *Gait.* Keep an eye on your Min Pin's gait, and watch for any signs of a limp.

If anything seems out of the ordinary, call your vet's office. They will tell you if it's time for you to bring your dog in, or whether it's something that you can wait out.

Fleas, Ticks, Heartworm, and Other Parasites

Parasites such as fleas, ticks, and heartworm can be threats to your dog on a year-long basis, and they can transmit diseases to your Min Pin.

Of all the parasites found in dogs, heartworms are the most deadly. Heartworms are carried by mosquitoes. If a dog is infected after being bitten by a carrier mosquito, the heartworms will grow inside the heart and into the large blood vessels of the lungs. While there are treatments available if your Min Pin is infected with heartworm disease, there can also be medical complications, high costs, and less than ideal situations (like months of required crate rest for your active Min Pin). Even after treatment, your Min Pin could be left with irreversible damage to his heart and lungs.

*Photo Courtesy
of Deb Mckillop*

Prevention is key to keep your dog from developing heartworm disease. Your vet can advise you as to what products and plans are best suited for your Min Pin. While these medications may seem expensive, year-round and consistent prevention is a much healthier and less expensive way to keep your Min Pin safe from the parasites he's bound to come into contact with.

FUN FACT
Champion Min Pin

While a Miniature Pinscher has never taken home the Best in Show title, the breed is well represented at the annual Westminster Kennel Club Dog Show. In 2019, the Miniature Pinscher Best of Breed champion was GCHS CH Kimro's One In A Minion, who was around three years old at the time, and the offspring of CH Kimro's Chase Manhattan and CH Kimro's Star Attraction.

Fleas can bite, transmit disease, and make your Min Pin itchy and miserable. They also suck blood when they bite, and this can cause your Min Pin to experience lethargy and weakness. They can also cause tapeworms and allergic dermatitis, as well as create a flea infestation in your entire home.

Like fleas (but usually bigger), ticks will suck your Min Pin's blood. Left unchecked, ticks can cause health problems, like Lyme disease, anaplasmosis, tick paralysis, and Rocky Mountain spotted fever.

To prevent fleas and ticks, you can use a year-round preventative medication. Some come as topical solutions, and others as pill-form. Talk to your vet about the right flea and tick preventative for your Min Pin.

Even when using tick preventative medications, it's still a good idea to check your Min Pin for ticks after time spent outside. You can simply comb through his fur with your fingers, and separate the fur and look closely if you feel anything that doesn't feel like his skin (like a bump or a swollen area). Make sure you check not just his torso, but also his head, neck, chin, ears, and between his toes. Remove any visible ticks you find with tweezers cleaned with isopropyl alcohol, making sure to remove the entire tick, and drop the tick in a solution of isopropyl alcohol and note the date you found the tick. Wash your hands, clean your Min Pin's wound with antiseptic, and clean your tweezers again with isopropyl alcohol.

Keep an eye on the area where the tick was to see if an infection surfaces. If the skin remains irritated or infected, or if your Min Pin starts showing signs of lethargy, swollen joints, fatigue, loss of appetite, or any other strange symptoms, make an appointment with your veterinarian.

Photo Courtesy
of Cynthia and Arthur Diaz

Vaccinations

When you first bring home your Min Pin, you will become very well acquainted with your veterinarian as you get up-to-date on all your pup's vaccinations. Like people, dogs need vaccines to prevent many diseases that are, quite often, without a cure. And dog vaccinations, like those for humans, sometimes require a booster to keep them effective. The best way to stay on schedule with vaccinations for your Min Pin is to follow the recommendations of your veterinarian.

Many vaccines can be given to dogs as young as 6 weeks old, so talk to your vet about setting up the best vaccination schedule for your Min Pin. These are the most common vaccines that your vet will recommend:

- **Bordetella Bronchiseptica**
  This bacteria can cause severe fits of coughing, whooping, vomiting, and, in rare cases, seizures and death. It's the primary cause of kennel cough. If you plan on boarding your puppy at a kennel, using dog daycare services, or attending group training classes, you will likely be required to show proof of this vaccination.

- **Rabies**
  Rabies is a severe viral disease that affects the brain and central nervous system. It's transmitted through bites from infected animals, and it's always fatal in dogs, with no treatment available. Prevention is key.

- **DHLPPC (combined vaccine for distemper, hepatitis, leptospirosis, parainfluenza, parvo, and corona)**
  This is often referred to as simply the "distemper shot." In actuality, this combination vaccine shot is protecting your dog from 6 different diseases. The two most important parts of this vaccine are distemper and parvo. Distemper shows in the form of flu-like symptoms, and can result in severe neurological symptoms and usually death. Parvo virus is airborne and spread through cough, sneezing, and stool. Parvo is also often deadly.

Holistic Alternatives

While seeing your veterinarian and keeping up with preventative care for your Min Pin is essential for his health, there may be other holistic alternatives available for you to help your Min Pin with certain issues or ailments.

Take Brady, for example. Later in his life, he had a bad tumble down the stairs when we were visiting his grandparents. He seemed okay after, but he had trouble getting out of bed in the morning (or after he'd been lying

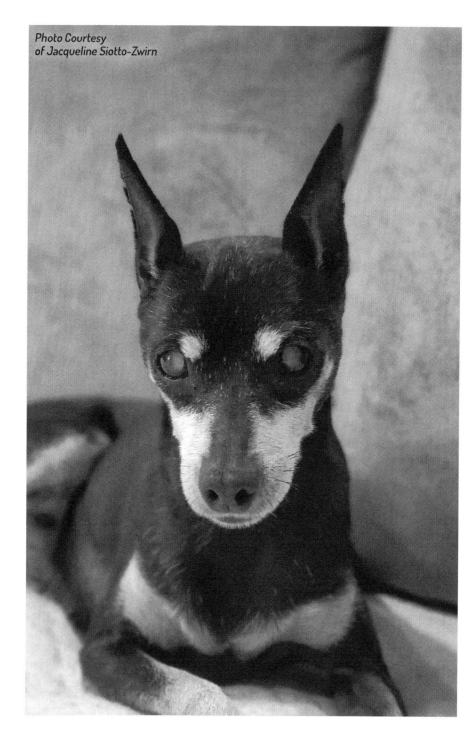

Photo Courtesy
of Jacqueline Siotto-Zwirn

down for an extended period of time). Instead of taking him to his regular vet, I called a holistic veterinarian that was recommended to me by a friend. She was a great fit for us because, while she was a trained veterinarian and could offer screenings and medications that any other veterinarian office could offer, she also had two additional "tools" under her toolbelt—acupuncture and chiropractic care for animals. As a human, I've experienced great benefits from both modalities of treatment, so I decided to give her a try. Within two visits of combined acupuncture and chiropractic treatments, Brady was back to himself—getting out of bed, walking, and running as if he didn't have a care in the world.

Here is a list of common holistic alternatives that you might explore for your Min Pin:

- *Acupuncture*
  Acupuncture is based on Traditional Chinese medicine. It involves inserting fine needles into specific areas on your dog's body to balance the flow of energy, or "chi." It's often used to control pain and chronic ailments.

- *Chiropractic care*
  A veterinarian that is trained in chiropractic care for dogs can provide hands-on spinal adjustments for your dog to relieve pain.

- *Herbal treatments & nutritional supplements*
  Herbal treatments use plant remedies to treat a variety of ailments. Nutritional supplements are intended to make up nutritional shortfalls in the diet by supplying extra vitamins, minerals, fatty acids, and amino acids. Make sure you talk to your vet before introducing any herbs to your Min Pin's diet.

- *Massage*
  Dog massage, like massage for humans, can lower the level of stress hormones in the body, increase circulation, and ease pain.

Always, always check with your veterinarian before you sign up for any holistic treatments or supplements to make sure they won't run counter to your Min Pin's preventative care and current medications.

Pet Insurance

Most pet parents pay out of pocket for their pets' medical expenses. But there is no way to anticipate what will happen in the future with your Min Pin's health. You certainly cannot predict when or how your Min Pin will get sick, or how much it will cost.

Regular veterinary care, wellness visits, and vaccines are a given cost, sure. But if your Min Pin comes down with an illness, your vet discovers something wrong at a wellness visit, there is a bad accident, or your Min Pin gets into a dog fight, these (and other) unforeseen expenses can add up. The average cost of an unexpected veterinary emergency can range anywhere from $800 to $1,500 (or more).

Photo Courtesy of Katja Koho

This is where pet insurance comes into play. Just like with human insurance policies, pet insurance policies can vary in terms of what they cover. Some plans are only good for vet costs if your Min Pin gets hurt or sick. Others will cover hereditary conditions like eye disorders, patellar luxation, etc., that are common to Min Pins. Some may cover alternative therapies, like acupuncture, chiropractic, and the like. And you might find one that covers behavioral conditions (e.g., pulling, destructive chewing, and excessive barking). You can also add coverage for preventative care (such as annual wellness exams, heartworm medications, dental cleaning, etc.).

Just like human insurance, you can find lower deductible and higher deductible options, differing copay amounts, etc. If you choose to get pet insurance, make sure you find one that (a) has everything you're looking for in terms of coverage, and (b) has the right copay and deductible program. And ask a few different insurance companies for quotes. Your veterinarian's office should have information on reliable, reputable pet insurance carriers that they can recommend.

CHAPTER 12

Caring for a Senior Miniature Pinscher

Basics of Senior Dog Care

As the years go by with your Min Pin, you might notice that he starts to slow down. Like people, Min Pins (and other dogs alike) can start to exhibit signs of one or more age-related conditions. These include a loss of hearing, a decline in vision, reduced mobility, and cognitive impairment. Other more serious conditions can arise, too, such as kidney disease or a heart condition.

Keeping up with your Min Pin's health from the time he is a puppy until he reaches his senior years is a good way to establish a baseline health problem and catch problems early. At your annual vet wellness exams, your vet will usually do some screening lab work—checking blood and stool samples

*Photo Courtesy
of Jacqueline Siotto-Zwirn*

for any irregularities. As time goes on, your vet can then compare results from year to year to identify any changes that might require treatment.

What are some of the things to expect as your Min Pin ages? He will probably slow down and require less exercise and playtime. He might tire more easily. He might have difficulty getting out of bed, hopping onto furniture, or moving up and down the stairs. He might have trouble seeing as well as he used to, or he might start showing signs of hearing loss.

FUN FACT
The Oldest Min Pin

Miniature Pinschers usually live anywhere from 12 to 16 years, on average, but how old is the oldest Min Pin on record? It's difficult to "pin" this number down. Some sources say that the oldest recorded Min Pin was 21 years old. Others claim that a Min Pin named Mickey, who was born in 1990, lived to be 25 years old. Yet another claim is that a woman named Jessica owned a Min Pin who lived to be 22 years old and died in 2013.

In addition to issues with hearing or vision, you might notice changes in your Min Pin's behavior. Maybe he'll bark at what seems to be nothing, or he'll start going to the bathroom in the house when he's previously been the best potty trained boy.

Whatever the signs of his decline, this is the time when your Min Pin needs your care and affection the most. As a dog owner, it is an incredibly hard thing to watch your little guy slow down. At the same time, it is when the deepest affection can run between you, because you both know, on some level, that your time is coming to a close.

About a year before Brady passed away, he began to slow down a lot. He wasn't up for long walks the way he used to be. He'd lie down if it was too hot. He'd turn back and head home if it was too cold. He stopped getting up into bed with me at night because the jump was too hard for him. He would walk into things that were in plain sight. And if I had him off-leash, he would lose me (because of his diminished sight and hearing), panic, and run in circles looking for me. It was devastating to watch, but it also endeared me to my little old man Min Pin even more because I knew how much he needed me to look after him.

This last chapter is meant to help guide you through the simple things of dealing with a senior dog. The things you can control—like his diet, his exercise, his dental care, his vet visits, etc.—are all things you can do to help your dog age well and increase his comfort level as he does.

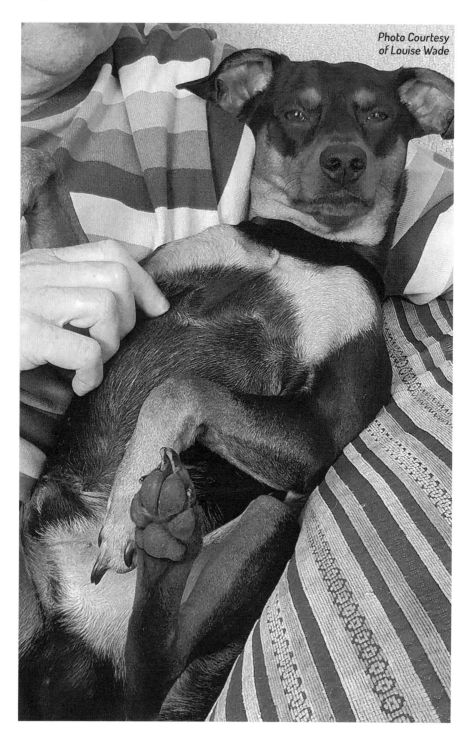

Photo Courtesy of Louise Wade

Nutrition

Just as when your Min Pin might have required a different food when he was a puppy, he might also need a different food as he graduates into his "senior" years, somewhere between age 7 and 9. Talk to your vet about which senior dog food is right. Your dog won't require as much protein as when he was an active little pup, but your senior Min Pin should get plenty of calcium and glucosamine to keep his joints and bones healthy.

You should also discuss with your vet adding fatty acids such as DHA and EPA to your senior Min Pin's diet. They have been shown to be useful for dogs with mobility issues due to arthritis or other joint diseases. Supplements including glucosamine and chondroitin are also beneficial for senior dogs.

If your senior Min Pin has any special conditions (like heart or kidney disease), your vet will recommend a special diet tailored to deal with that.

Make sure you work with your vet to keep your Min Pin at his ideal weight as he ages. Overweight dogs tend to have a higher incidence of diseases like diabetes, heart disease, skin disease, or cancer. Keeping your senior Min Pin fed well, and at a good weight, will hopefully keep him by your side for longer!

Exercise

It may seem counterintuitive that as your Min Pin slows down and is less inclined for longer walks and rigorous play, exercise will become even more important. But the reason for this is that exercise will keep your senior Min Pin lean and healthy, and help him maintain healthy joints and muscles.

You'll need to tailor your Min Pin's exercise as he ages and has different needs. Let's say you're used to taking one long walk with him during the day, but now he only wants to go for one or two blocks at a time. You can shorten his walks, and add extra short-distance walks and play sessions throughout the day to keep him moving.

You'll also need to be careful with your senior Min Pin on hotter days. Just like old people can't tolerate heat as well, the same goes for dogs. Make sure you keep him hydrated and indoors on days when the heat index is high, and keep walks short enough to let him do his business and go home. On those days, you can add in extra indoor play sessions if your pup is up for it!

And remember to keep your Min Pin mentally stimulated. While he might not be up for long physical excursions, he would benefit from play and puzzle time, just like he did when he was a pup. Play hide and seek, try out new puzzle toys, or even work on teaching your Min Pin new commands. These types of activity keep your Min Pin engaged and tire him out without strenuous exercise.

Photo Courtesy
of Robert Bienvenu

Common Old-Age Ailments

As your Min Pin ages, you'll start to notice a lot of gradual changes. Some of these changes (like him going gray in spots) may be benign; others might be a sign of a more serious condition. The most common old-age ailments your Min Pin might encounter, and how you can deal with them, are below:

- **Arthritis**
  Arthritis is when the cartilage that protects joint surfaces wears down over time. Signs that your Min Pin is developing arthritis include reluctance to climb stairs, stiffness in the morning or after long periods of rest, and limping. To help reduce the impact of aging on your Min Pin's joints, it is important to make sure your Min Pin stays at a healthy weight so there isn't too much of a heavy load on his joints. You can also talk to your vet for food and/or supplement suggestions to help with his mobility.

- **Dental Disease**
  Dental disease is common in all senior dogs. It can be painful, causing your Min Pin to avoid eating or have difficulty eating his meals, which can lead to weight loss and an unkempt hair coat. Dental disease can also cause tooth loss and bacteria in the bloodstream that can damage internal organs. You can help prevent dental disease with regular tooth brushing, as well as specialized foods that are intended to promote dental health. As your Min Pin ages, your vet may recommend regular (yearly) dental cleanings at the veterinary clinic.

- **Hearing Loss**
  As your Min Pin ages, his hearing will likely start to diminish. Signs that he can't hear as well as he used to include if: your Min Pin doesn't come when you call him, he doesn't respond to noises inside or out of the house the same way that he used to, or he startles easily when you approach him from behind. There isn't much to do about hearing loss, except learn how to communicate with your Min Pin by letting him see you, using hand gestures, and always keeping him on leash when you're outdoors.

- **Sight Issues**
  As your Min Pin ages, you might notice his eyes getting cloudy or blue-colored. This isn't always a sign of sight loss. However, if there is a white cloud over your Min Pin's pupil, it could mean that he has cataracts, which would cause some diminished sight. If you notice your Min Pin walking into things that are in plain sight, not being able to see treats on the floor, or he shows signs of anxiety when he's in unfamiliar settings, check with your vet. Some sight issues (like cataracts) can be

*Photo Courtesy
of Karis Antokal*

helped with surgery; others are just something you might need to deal with as your Min Pin ages.

- **Obesity**
Obesity is an issue for a lot of senior dogs, and that increase in weight can lead to a number of other problems, like joint disease, diabetes, and respiratory illness. Exercise and managing your Min Pin's diet are the key to managing his weight. Since, as he ages, he'll be less active, your Min Pin's diet will also have to change. Regular, gentle exercise will be beneficial for your Min Pin to stay at a healthy weight as he ages.

- **Hypothyroidism**
If your Min Pin is overweight, but he's been on a vet-approved weight loss plan without success, it's possible that he might have hypothyroidism (an underactive thyroid, which results in a sluggish metabolism). Hypothyroidism can be diagnosed by your vet with a simple blood test and regulated with medication.

- **Cancer**
Dogs are susceptible to many types of cancer, much like humans. Signs that your Min Pin could have cancer include lumps or bumps underneath his skin; abnormal odors coming from his mouth, ears, or any other part of the body; abnormal discharge from his eyes, mouth, ears, or rectum; abdominal swelling; wounds or sores that just won't heal; sudden and irreversible weight loss; or changes in appetite. Call your vet if any of these symptoms appear, since early detection and diagnosis is the key for your Min Pin to survive cancer.

- **Urinary Incontinence**
Older dogs may exhibit loss of bladder control, or incontinence. There are many potential causes, including hormonal imbalance, urinary tract infections, loss of muscle tone, or spinal injuries. If you think your Min Pin is incontinent, call your vet to find out the cause and the right treatment.

This list of common aging ailments is not exhaustive, and it's also not meant to exhaust you. It's good to be prepared for your Min Pin's aging process, but the important piece is to stay present and enjoy your Min Pin while you can. Keep your vet involved at every step so he stays healthy, call your vet if anything seems amiss, and spend as much time as you can loving the little old man your Min Pin has become.

Navigating Steps and Bare Floors

As your Min Pin ages, you might notice that he can't navigate steps or bare floors as well as he used to. Brady would do this cartoon-like skid where all of his limbs started scurrying at the same time, and when that didn't work, he'd go "splat" on his belly. It was both absolutely adorable and horrifying to watch at the same time. To help him out, I put down extra area rugs so that he could get the grip he needed to navigate my slick hardwood floors.

He also had a hard time navigating stairs. Climbing up and down stairs can be precarious for older dogs who have muscle loss or weakness in their legs. Their reduced ability to push themselves up or to support their weight coming down stairs can lead to slips and stumbles, especially on non-carpeted staircases. You can get some non-slip stair treads to try first. If that doesn't help your Min Pin, you can start carrying him up and down the stairs. The great thing about Min Pins is they are so small and portable, you can easily carry them. You can become your Min Pin's personal escalator! He will feel like the regal King of Toys he was always meant to be.

If you notice your Min Pin is having trouble with stairs, you'll also want to put gates at the top of stair landings so your Min Pin doesn't try to navigate them on his own. It'll also help prevent inadvertent falls down the stairs if your dog starts to lose his sight.

Enjoying Your Time Together

This chapter is probably going to be hard for you to read because you won't want to imagine your time with your Min Pin is winding down, or that he might suffer as his body ages. I know it's been challenging for me to write because the end of my days with Brady were both some of the most joyful of our times together, and they were also the most challenging.

Watching the Min Pin that you love somehow turn into this ancient, old dog who can't see, can't hear, loses footing, and becomes ill can be absolutely devastating. You remember the days when he was full of energy and always excited to see you with his crazy, puppy-like antics, but the reality of his senior days is that he spends much of them sleeping. When he's awake, he eats, he plays a little, and he's happy to see you. But then he's very happy to retreat into a resting, lazy state, and you, as his owner, his parent, and his best friend—you have to watch and know that your days together are coming to a close.

Brady and I moved together a lot. We lived in Manhattan. We lived in Pennsylvania. We lived in various apartments in various places, and we traveled and hiked a lot. As he got into his last year of life, I felt something in him say: "Stop, Mom. Slow down. I need to rest." So I found an apartment that had an elevator and a park down the street, and we moved into what I told all my friends was going to be Brady's old folks' home. I knew that this was the last of our time together, and so did he.

During your Min Pin's senior years, my advice to you is: enjoy every moment you have together. Don't spend the time thinking about how youthful he used to be and how much fun you used to have together. Find ways to enjoy each other fully now. There's a tenderness that will unfold between you as your Min Pin ages in his life. He will sense that he is even more dependent on you than he's ever been, and you will know that the only reason he's hanging around is to watch over you and make sure you'll be okay without him.

Enjoy every play session, every walk, every time you get to snuggle with one another or hold hands (his paw in your hand) will be a blessing if you let it. Wake up each day and say, "Thank you for another day with my best friend."

Saying Goodbye

When age or illness dramatically changes your Min Pin's ability to function in his day-to-day activities, you will be asked to start thinking about your Min Pin's quality of life. Are the aging signs you're seeing enough to warrant euthanizing your best friend? Or is it something he can live happily with until he is ready to go on his own?

Some of the more troubling signs include the inability to breathe normally, to eat or drink, or to even perform routine tasks like getting up to walk to the food or water bowl or go outside to relieve himself. In those instances, your vet and your family members may urge you to consider euthanasia. If your pup isn't eating or drinking, he's not wagging his tail, or you can tell he is in a lot of pain, it is definitely a sign that something is wrong.

Brady's decline came on suddenly. He had slowed down, yes, but he was still enjoying life—eating, drinking, playing, and taking shorter walks—until one day, when I found one of Brady's teeth on the floor in my apartment. I wasn't overly concerned because Brady had already had some dental issues, but I called my vet anyway. They did some routine bloodwork to see whether they could put him under anesthesia to remove the remaining piece of the tooth, and it was then that we realized something was the matter: his liver enzymes were elevated. They suggested I take him to a specialist, so I set up the appointment right away. And within a few days of seeing the specialist and two emergency trips to the vet, I had no choice but to put him down. He had developed significant levels of pain, so much so that he would pace for hours in circles and then hide in a corner, while wailing and crying. The

Photo Courtesy
of Hege Isabella

veterinarians he saw (including the specialist) weren't sure whether he had developed something called hepatic encephalopathy (a neurological condition related to his decreased liver function), or whether he had slipped a disc in his neck. But either way, the signs were not good for a recovery, and aside from doping him up with morphine, there wasn't an end in sight to his pain. It was horrible to watch and experience alongside him.

There was a moment where he was lying with me, and I just felt something within him say to me, "Mom, it's time to let me go." And so I did. I called the vet, and they gave him a very respectful and respectable send-off. He died in my arms, beautifully and at peace.

There is absolutely nothing easy about letting your Min Pin leave you. Whether you've been together 5 years or 15, that pup is a part of you. He is your heart, your best friend, and your forever companion. And somehow, you have to muster the courage to say goodbye to him.

If it were up to us humans, our pets would never leave us. But at some point, you have to weigh the pros and cons and ask yourself: Is this the life I want for my pup? Is he suffering? Am I keeping him around only for me? Ask your vet, ask your family members, and ask your close friends. Ultimately, though, you have to ask your Min Pin: Are you ready to go?

Whether you decide to euthanize your Min Pin or wait for him to exit his body on his own, there will also be choices you'll need to make: burial (at home or in a pet cemetery), cremation, whether you want to save the ashes, etc. Make sure you have someone there to support you as you make these decisions, because in those moments you may not be thinking clearly.

And when you do have to say goodbye, continue treasuring the time you had with your Min Pin. Honor his life by honoring the good times you had together.

Brady and I had so many adventures together. Hiking, exploring, and laughing with one another in every situation in life. When I met Brady, already a senior dog, he stole my heart. He brought me so much laughter, so much joy, and so much love at a time in my life when I didn't have much of it. He was my sidekick for five and a half years, and he lit up the hearts of everyone he met. I am so incredibly grateful that Brady came into my life, and I'm so incredibly grateful that I can share his story with you.

Just know this: even though your Min Pin's days may be winding to a close, he will forever live on in your heart.

Made in the USA
Monee, IL
23 September 2022

14516777R00068